D0195030

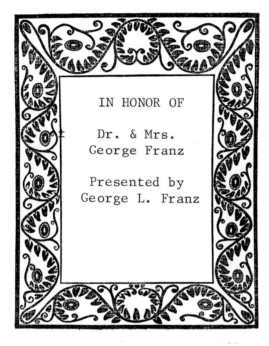

IN HONOR OF

Dr. & Mrs.
George Franz

Presented by
George L. Franz

RELIGION IN PLANETARY PERSPECTIVE

RELIGION IN PLANETARY PERSPECTIVE

A Philosophy of Comparative Religion

William W. Mountcastle, Jr.

WITHDRAWN

Abingdon
Nashville

RELIGION IN PLANETARY PERSPECTIVE:
A PHILOSOPHY OF COMPARATIVE RELIGION

Library of Congress Cataloging in Publication Data

Mountcastle, William W   1925-
  Religion in planetary perspective.

  Bibliography: p.
  1. Religion—Study and teaching. 2. Religion—
Philosophy. I. Title.
BL41.M64   200'.7   77-17111

ISBN 0-687-36023-4

Cover design, illustration, and calligraphy by Billie Jean Osborne and author.

MANUFACTURED BY THE PARTHENON PRESS AT
NASHVILLE, TENNESSEE, UNITED STATES OF AMERICA

For Ila

All the religions in the world, like all the women in the world, do not compare with the one that is our own.

—Radhakrishnan

Preface

For a number of years I have been privileged to teach courses in both philosophy and religion. The combination of the rich content of the great religions with the critical analysis of the philosophic tradition has been a constant stimulation and challenge to my students and to me. It has also become just as clear that some teachers and students have not had the opportunity to experience this kind of synthesis. Philosophy of religion is often taught in a kind of antiseptic vacuum and biblical religion is learned as if it were the only religion on planet Earth! Even when the other great religions are studied, the approach is often more descriptive than analytical and critical.

My students and I felt the need for a more holistic, synoptic approach to the critical study of religion. Out of countless sessions—formal classroom meetings and informal encounters—the present book was fashioned. It is an attempt to introduce the reader—both the formal student and the interested general reader—to the critical study of the major themes and problems expounded by the great religions. Of course, it builds upon foundations already laid by scholars in the fields of individual religions, comparative religion, theology and philosophy of religion. The underlying idea is that for too long a time scholars in these several disciplines have been ignoring—or worse disparaging—the findings and insights of their colleagues. This kind of autonomy serves no one, and the philosophy of comparative religion declares that it must be supplemented by a synoptic overview.

Notice, I say "supplemented," indicating that there will always be a need for the pure specialist. It is the specialist who provides us with the details that are absolutely necessary for significant learning. But an important goal of education is to learn to view the parts as belonging to a coherent whole. With this idea in mind, I offer the philosophy of comparative religion as a method of correlating the categories of philosophical analysis with the essential data from the great religions. The goal is to reach a clearer understanding that will enable us to make value judgments concerning the truth claims of the world religions. Moreover, special problems relevant to our new approach will be selected, and solutions suggested. The intention is to remain true to the philosophic spirit of free and open inquiry and not to flinch when it comes to stating a value judgment that appears to have been earned by "good reasons."

Not everyone will accept the conclusions and some may even be greatly disturbed. But this has been the price of philosophic inquiry for a good while. It may also be the reason this particular project has been so long in surfacing. But if truth is indeed One and we hope to find a way to live together on planet Earth, there seems to be no good reason for putting off a philosophy of comparative religion any longer.

The general reader should, perhaps, be reminded that no philosopher worth his salt makes a claim to omniscience and that a sense of humor is quite as important for serious inquiry as are the logical laws. I hope this book will stimulate earnest dialogue and serious rebuttal. It is only a beginning—an introduction to the philosophy of comparative religion.

As I think back on my own student days, I recall exciting times with great teachers to whom I am very much indebted. Those who come immediately to mind are Professors Milo Connick, Elmer Leslie, Harold DeWolf, Peter Bertocci, Paul Schilling, Paul Tillich, and Alan Watts. I wish to give special thanks to Dr. Bertocci, who has given me much encouragement and was kind enough to read portions of the manuscript and offer valuable suggestions. Of course, the conclusions are my own; I can hold no others responsible.

Any teacher must also be sensitive to the invaluable suggestions that have come from his students, and I remember my students and am thankful for their rich contribution to my growth as a scholar and teacher. My thanks also go to Ileana Reamsma who typed the glossary and index and to Linda Archer who very painstakingly typed the entire manuscript.

Contents

Introduction

The beautiful color image of planet Earth flashing on our television screens delivered a culture shock that dramatically altered our self-image. From that moment on, many realized that it would never again be possible to correctly assess the value of any phenomenon without seeing it as part of a total pattern, so dramatically symbolized by the floating blue-and-white marbeled planet. In tune with this general awareness of wholeness which seems to characterize the dawning space age, philosophers are awakening from the mesmerizing spell cast upon them by analytic philosophy and recovering their vision of synoptic truth. Theologians and students of particular religious traditions have also been opening their minds to important aspects of traditions other than their own.

The focus of the present essay is religion—the religion of humankind on planet Earth. This is clearly a proper topic for religious studies, but as our intention is to employ categories of critical analysis, it will also be a philosophical and theological inquiry. Unfortunately, a strange mixture of prejudice and misunderstanding often places traditional philosophy of religion, theology, and conventional religious studies in hostile camps, and we fail to recognize and appropriate data and methodologies which would help us develop a more comprehensive and coherent approach to the study of religion. With respect to the topic of religion in planetary perspective, the most appropriate disciplines from the religious studies are in-depth studies of individual religious traditions, comparative religion and theology, and from the side of philosophy, it is the philosophy of religion. Those who are familiar with these disciplines are aware of certain limitations that can be identified by briefly sketching each of these approaches to the study of religion.

The philosophy of religion is concerned with analyzing several facets of the religious phenomenon for the triple purposes of clarification, explication, and verification. Problems usually included concern the sources of religious knowledge with questions about the relationship of faith to reason and criteria of truth, assessment of the data of religious experience, the function of religious language and criteria of meaning, arguments and counterarguments for the existence of God, the problems of suffering and evil, and speculation about the destiny of persons after death. Philosophers of religion are distinguished from theologians by their attempt to be more objective. They make it a point to stand outside the circle of faith, believing that this will lend greater credibility to their conclusions. At just this point, however, the philosopher of religion may very well miss the sort of data which are available only to one who knows the meaning of a faith commitment. This, of course, refers to the subjective perspective on knowledge which Søren Kierkegaard insisted was fundamental to finding religious truth.

There is another deficiency that may be even more significant for the doing of space-age philosophy. A careful examination of the content of traditional philosphy of religion reveals a theistic focus clearly stamped in the Western mold. Questions about the nature of God, divine revelation, and the possibility of existence after death are usually framed in the categories of traditional interpretations the biblical legacy. Admittedly, in recent years there has been an attempt to include non-Western perspectives and, typically, this is accomplished in a philosophy of religion text structured as a book of readings featuring, perhaps, an article on Zen and another relating to Chinese or Indian religious philosophy. But these unique points of view are not adequately correlated with traditional Western perspectives, and they remain stepchildren

14

representing a kind of philosophical tokenism. This approach to understanding religion does not seem to be adequate if we assume a planetary perspective.

When we turn to what is generally called comparative religion we find that our objections of parochialism and ethnocentrism have been met, as the chief purpose of this discipline is to identify salient features of and the history of each of the great world religions. This discipline shares with philosophy an objective attitude, but it is guided more by the model of the social sciences, which stresses description, than by philosophical method with its critical analysis and normative criteria. The objectivity of comparative religion is often balanced by subjective views obtained by including essays from the perspectives of members of the various faiths, thereby meeting our earlier objection leveled against the exclusively objective philosophical approach. This developing science of religion has added much to our fund of knowledge about the great world religions, particularly with regard to the historical and sociological dimensions, but it sometimes lacks the rigor of philosophical analysis, the maturity of philosophical evaluation, and the imagination and sensitivity of the best contemporary theology. But if it is predominantly a fact-finding social science, its ecumenical scope makes it one that is uniquely well suited for this age of global awareness.

Intensive study of the individual religions, particularly the faiths rooted in the Old and New Testaments, has produced significant results. Textual, historical, form and redaction criticism, give us more accurate translations and more imaginative understanding of scripture. Archaeological discoveries and a growing appreciation of ancient Mideastern civilizations help to increase our understanding of the origin and early development of Judaism and Christianity. This kind of detailed analysis of every scriptural passage in the context of an overview of the developing faith must form the foundation for any serious study of religion. Of course, its weakness is that generally scholars in a particular religious tradition are quite innocent of significant and perhaps parallel ideas in other religions. This is especially apparent when we compare the work of New Testament exegetes with that of Indian and Chinese scholars.

The theologians are concerned with explicating and providing reasonable defense for the doctrines of a particular religion. Their

15

task requires that, among other things, they have an adequate grasp of the work done by the scholars who labor in the areas of "lower" and "higher" biblical criticism. If they are doing systematic or philosophical theology they must also be aware of philosophical problems relevant to religious matters and develop their work in terms of philosophical method. Though modern theologians seem to be well aware of work done in the field of biblical scholarship and are often quite sophisticated with regard to borrowing and adapting ideas from other disciplines for their use, e.g., existential and psychological insights that suggest ways of understanding the doctrine of original sin, they have not, generally, been quick to recognize certain contributions by the analytical philosophers. Theologians could, of course, return the compliment by pointing out that the linguistic analysis of philosophers could profit by drawing upon the usually ignored insights stemming from the new hermeneutic.

It is the thesis of the present study that each of the disciplines identified possesses unique strengths that could be dramatically reinforced through a synthesis that would also neutralize their weaknesses. This new discipline we propose to call the philosophy of comparative religion. The philosophical, theological, and exegetical techniques of clarification, critical analysis, and synoptic viewing of empirical data provided by the great world religions will establish the foundation for the proper identification, evaluation, and possible resolution of religious problems relevant to the religious experiences and philosophies of man from a global perspective.

The procedure to be followed in this attempt to develop a philosophy of comparative religion will have two main parts. Part 1 will develop the procedure, beginning in chapter 2, by identifying categories of philosophical and theological analysis. The first category will identify the philosophical and religious questions that are useful in explicating the subject matter offered by the great world religions. The second category will be that of clarification and will focus on the problem of religious language, surveying several theories of its use and the various kinds of meaning which that unique language can convey. The third category will be verification and will discuss methods of evaluating the truth value of religious assertions. Tests involving logical criteria long associated with traditional philosophy will be identified, but attention will also be given to special problems more recently posed by existential and phenomenological insights such as the subjective factors of mood, attitude, and illumination. Questions about the relativity of truth and the possibility of syncretism will also be considered.

In chapter 3, the second step will be to present the data offered by the several great religions. Clearly we must be selective at this point to avoid becoming lost in a jungle of data, much of which would be quite irrelevant for our purpose. Much interesting and valuable material of a largely historical, cultural, or aesthetic sort would not add measurably to a critique that is primarily analytical. The task will be to distill the essence from each of the several traditions selected and present only those propositions that express the quintessence of each faith. In a departure from the procedure of comparative religion, we will not try to summarize each religion as a distinct entity, but rather group the ideas under headings more appropriate to a philosophical study. We will work with the following models: cosmic naturalism, spiritual monism, and personalistic theism.

The third step, chapter 4, will involve correlating the essential insights of the great religions with the criteria of explication and then applying the criteria of clarification and verification for the very difficult and serious purpose of evaluating their truth claims. An attempt will be made to identify the parameters of religious truth as found in the data and construct a philosophical model. It is neither the thesis nor the intent of the present inquiry to construct this model to serve as a prophecy or a guide for the religion of the future. That sort of activity belongs properly to the mystic and the seer. The model we propose will serve as a provisional norm useful for doing the philosophy of comparative religion with respect to evaluating problems and solutions pertaining to specific areas of inquiry.

Part II will present examples of doing the philosophy of comparative religion in terms of three special problems that appear to be unique to this new discipline. The first problem will begin with a recognition of the triadic themes found in the major religions and attempt to offer an explanation for this phenomenon. The second problem will consider the nature of ultimate reality as perceived by the several religions in terms of a continuum of possibilities ranging from monism to theism. The third problem will focus on the status of persons and consider the range of possibilities ranging from reality to illusion and finite to infinite models.

The goal of this procedure that we have detailed is nothing less than to develop a new discipline, which we have identified as the philosophy of comparative religion. Our aim is to establish the foundation for this new approach to the study of religion and then demonstrate its value by giving examples showing how it can be used to clarify and resolve important religious and philosophical problems from a global perspective. While a course specifically developed for the philosophy of comparative religion would certainly be the most appropriate use for this volume, it would seem that students in the traditional disciplines of philosophy of religion, comparative religion, and theology would find in this new perspective an exciting way to enrich and bring balance to their venerable areas of study.

We should also note that our aim is to develop every step of our analysis with clarity, giving elementary background material where it seems appropriate, so that the interested lay reader can also follow the unfolding of the ideas. The inclusion of Sanskrit, Chinese calligraphy, Hebrew, and Greek should not be seen as forbidding but as an exciting invitation. It has been included for the purpose of clarification and to dramatically emphasize the vital importance of language in any serious philosophical analysis and especially for the study of religion. The role of intuition and aesthetic perception is no less important than intellectual apprehension, though many professional Western scholars seem to have overlooked this. The "metaphysical illustrations" are also intended to summarize and communicate through aesthetic categories what is developed by rational analysis.

Part I: Developing a New Approach to Religion

Chapter One:
The Emerging Vision:
Background Studies in
Comparative Philosophy

A new idea has been emerging since the first quarter of the present century when Albert Schweitzer wrote his *Philosophy of Civilization* in 1923 and has received additional impetus from the work of Radhakrishnan and C. E. Moore in 1939. At first thought, it might appear that these efforts belong properly to the study of comparative religion founded by Max Müller a century ago, but closer inspection reveals the use of critical philosophical categories, which suggests and perhaps presages our proposed philosophy of comparative religion. The thesis of the present study is that these valuable earlier efforts do not meet the requirements of our proposed new discipline but are more correctly regarded as examples of the philosophy of culture. Nevertheless, it is fitting that we survey these earlier studies and build the new discipline on such data and insights as they may provide.

The Philosophy of Civilization, **Schweitzer**

Schweitzer's initial insight is that the optimistic philosophy of the West stands in opposition to the pessimistic philosophy of the East as the two strive to imprint their own distinctive mark on the "world philosophy" which is just dawning. In his view, Chinese and Indian philosophy must "solve the problem of how far we can recognize the original source of the world as ethical, and how far, correspondingly, we become ethical by the surrender to it of our will." In opposition to this monistic world view stands the ethical dualism of Western religious philosophy, which assumes the existence of two world principles—the natural and the ethical. In contrast to the Chinese and Indians, the ethical dualists seek not harmony with nature in the cosmic will that grounds it but harmony with the ethical divine Person "outside and above the world." Their optimism stems from their unshakable conviction "that ethical force will prove superior to natural, and so raise the world and mankind to true perfection."[1]

Eastern thought finds an echo in the monistic systems of Hegel and Schopenhauer. Hegel's thought, like that of Vedanta, concludes that the ultimate meaning of the world can be expressed only in intellectual rather than in ethical terms. Schweitzer observes that "both give value to ethics only as a phase of intellectuality."[2] Schopenhauer's philosophy receives even harsher judgment because his premise of world and life negation makes all ethical actions illusory. Perhaps most penetrating of all Schweitzer's critical observations is his charge that "Schopenhauer's pity, like that of the Brahmans and the Buddha, is at bottom merely theoretical. It can use as its own the words of the religion of love, but it stands at a far lower level. As in the case with the thinkers of India, the ideal of inactivity obstructs the way to the real ethics of love."[3]

Schweitzer's second basic insight involves his perception that mysticism grounds both an intellectual world and life view and the ethic of self-perfecting. But the relationship between ethics and mysticism is not at all obvious either to Eastern or Western thinkers. Indian thought sees clearly the distinction and "with the most varied phrasing it repeats the proposition: 'Spirituality is not ethics.' " Spirituality, observes Schweitzer, is not ethics; indeed, mysticism devours ethics![4] Western religious thought also maintains this distinction, and it is precisely this that accounts for the shallow quality of much Western activism.

But the premise that mysticism does ground all true ethics holds, and the problem is to find the key to solving the paradox.

Schweitzer believes the trouble lies in a false mysticism which mistakes abstractionism about reality for Being itself. "There is no Essence of Being, but only infinite Being in infinite manifestations." This is the lesson for the East. The West needs to experience the honest mystical insight that "I am life which wills to live, in the midst of life which wills to live." When the nerve of ethical sensitivity is thereby stimulated, and we are moved to devotion of our being to infinite Being in all its manifestations, we will suddenly realize that "the gruesome truth that spirituality and ethics are two different things no longer holds good. Here the two are one and the same." It is this recognition of the union of true mysticism with ethics that grounds Schweitzer's famous dictum "reverence for life." "Reverence for life means to be in the grasp of the infinite, inexplicable, forward-urging Will in which all Being is grounded." "Ethics consists," concludes Schweitzer, "in my experiencing the compulsion to show all will-to-live the same reverence as I do my own."[5]

Clearly, Schweitzer's insights as to the main characteristics found in the religions of East and West and his imaginative solution to the problem of reconciling the values found in mysticism with the value of an ethical world view carry us beyond the traditional study called comparative religion. We will want to give careful attention to the possibility of incorporating his conclusions into the philosophy of comparative religion. But this work, taken as a whole, really goes beyond the scope of philosophy of comparative religion and is more correctly identified as a philosophy of culture or philosophy of civilization as Schweitzer, himself, titles it. Much space is devoted to the details of Western philosophy, but it is focused on Schweitzer's main concern to study world views with special attention given the ethical dimension.

The philosophy of comparative religion should give more attention to questions about ultimate reality, the status of the person, and questions about values in a more balanced way. This will be the substance of part II of our project. In order to do this properly, greater attention must be given to specific manifestions and details of Chinese and Indian thought as well as Western religion. Certainly, Schweitzer is aware of these details as his other work clearly demonstrates, but he does not choose to incorporate

23

them and integrate them for the purpose of achieving a detailed and systematic comparative study.

Mysticism East and West, **Otto**

This exercise in comparative religion is focused on the phenomenon of mysticism and further defined to draw almost exclusively on the work of Shankara and Eckhart.[6] Both these masters are more theologians than philosophers since their interest lies in obtaining the religious goal of salvation rather than theoretical knowledge for its own sake. Yet, they both agree that knowledge is the way to salvation; and paradoxically, they would both finally admit that they really have no method to offer! Yoga may be a preparation for Shankara just as Eckhart recognizes the *methodus mystica;* but, these are not blueprints for finding ultimate reality.[7]

Both would agree that as valuable as logic is as a tool for clarifying the understanding and exposing fallacies, it can never find Brahman or God. Eckhart distinguishes between *intellectus*—the faculty whereby we intuit transcendental truth—and *ratio*—the faculty of discursive, conceptual understanding. Similarly, Shankara distinguishes between the authority of *Sruti,* or scripture, and mere human reasoning, or *anumana.*[8] These details are important for our project because they show how the conventional approach of philosophy of religion, which considers reason and faith, must be expanded to include mystical illumination and what theologians call the new hermeneutic. This technical term refers to an approach to scripture that allows for the possibility that religious truth might be discerned as the language of the text affects the sympathetic reader rather than discovered by examining the text as an object. Of this we shall have more to say in the next chapter.

Otto singles out four distinct categories with which to illustrate significant differences between Eastern and Western religious philosophy. Shankara's concept of Brahman seems to be closer to static Being or "resting *Sat* " than to the infinite process, which is Eckhart's vision of God. Such expressions of Eckhart's as " 'a wheel rolling out of itself,' 'a stream flowing into itself' . . . are metaphors which would be quite impossible for the One of Sankara." Of the Western concept of God, Otto observes: "This

God is in Himself a living *process,* not a static Being."[9] To be the "living God" is something quite different from "the God who lives."

With respect to the relation of God to the world, Otto remarks that for Shankara, the coming forth of God and the world from the primeval oneness of Brahman is the great mistake, or *avidya,* but for Eckhart the activity of God in nature and persons is a fact full of meaning and value. Here is the opportunity for life to achieve the fullness of its potentiality!

Otto finds that the passive-active difference between Eastern and Western philosophy carries over into two models of the soul. Shankara develops the idea of the soul coming home to perfect contentment and rest in Brahman, while Eckhart sees a restless soul that "seeks God with rage" and is "never 'there,' never in a final static rest."[10] This view, in Otto's judgment, is neither Indian nor Plotinian but Gothic. A student of the Old Testament reflecting on the study of Jacob's wrestling match with the angel of God, might suggest that it is Hebrew! Shankara's *atman* is not the Christian soul "infinitely rich in life and depth, a place of ever fuller experience and possession."[11] These conclusions of Otto's regarding the nature of God and the soul need a more detailed and sustained analysis, and we will deal with this in part 2, chapters 6 and 7.

Finally, Otto believes he has discovered a radical difference that reminds us of Schweitzer's earlier observations. Specifically, Shankara is so concerned with the subjective dimension of salvation that the human community is all but ignored. The fourteenth section, sixteenth chapter of the Chandogya Upanishad which describes the all-consuming desire of a lost soul to "return home" to Brahman is cited. There is no passion for righteousness such as we find in Matt. 5:6: "Blessed are those who hunger and thirst after righteousness, for they shall be satisfied." While Indian thought focuses upon escape from *samsara,* Western religion is deeply concerned with gaining victory over injustice and seeing righteousness triumph. Otto quotes a stunning verse from Eckhart: "The righteous men take righteousness so earnestly that were God not righteous, they would not care a jot for Him."[12]

Otto explains this by noting that for Eckhart, when we achieve unity with the righteous Being, we acquire righteousness which

25

then permeates all our living. This living activity of the "new obedience" is a kind of "mysticism of the will" that overcomes the "mysticism of Being." In sharp contrast stands Shankara's view that the ethics of the Gita serve only as a prologue for the final mystical state of unity with Brahman—a state removed from all works, both good and evil. Works always bind us and we seek to leave them behind that we may repose in oneness. But this Indian view is not immoral; it is simply amoral. This, Otto concludes, is "because it springs not from the soil of Palestine, but from the soil of India."[13] Surely, this mystical observation will need to be explained and defended in less metaphorical language. But we owe much to Otto for helping break new ground in the study of comparative religious philosophy, and certain of his insights will receive further attention in the course of our analysis.

Eastern Religions and Western Thought, **Radhakrishnan**

Radhakrishnan announces that the study of comparative religion "has broken down the barriers behind which dogmatists seek to entrench themselves and show that their own religion is unique." But conflict and competition will continue unless we develop a "spirit of comprehension which will break down prejudice and misunderstanding and bind them together as varied expressions of a single truth." He is in agreement with Schweitzer with respect to the prime importance of the mystical experience in all religions. He finds a "remarkable unity of spirit" with regard to mystics of the different religions and believes that "all signs indicate that it is likely to be the religion of the future."[14]

Radhakrishnan is also in agreement with Schweitzer regarding the key role an ethical life view plays in achieving the goal of reconciliation. "By raising the standard of religious life we clarify the vision"[15]; that is, each and every religion must participate in the self-reform that involves reinterpretation and adjustment to one another in the course of pursuing the ethical life.

He disagrees sharply, however, with Schweitzer's contention that the Indian view is pessimistic and nonsupportive of an ethical life view. In fact, for Radhakrishnan, Hinduism is the key to unlocking the mystery surrounding conflicting religious views, because it is "the most elastic of all religions, the most capable of adapting itself to new conditions. It is less dependent on historical facts, is freer from authority. Its gods form no exclusive group." It is in this tradition that Radhakrishnan finds the twin virtues of loyalty to the truth as one understands it and the spirit of inquiry: devotion to the truth which is larger than any single tradition. Then, "religious life becomes a co-operative enterprise binding together different traditions and perspectives to the end of attaining a clearer vision of the perfect reality."[16]

In fact, Radhakrishnan finds Western religion suffers a great ethical deficiency. While those who believe in an immanent Logos should recognize the indwelling divine spirit in other religions, quite the contrary is often the case. "This whole order of ideas derived from the Logos doctrine is wrecked by the Jewish inheritance. For the Jews Yahweh was the God, and all other gods were the gods of their enemies." By contrast, Hinduism is much more ethical because, recognizing divine immanence, its concept of the "chosen people" embraces all humankind.[17]

Islam, another Western religion, has also exhibited ethical deficiencies, but "the dogmatism of Islam was toned down by India."[18] Radhakrishnan recounts the interesting story of the emperor Akbar who modifies his absolutistic Moslem faith and is brought to see that there are values in all religions and that it is impossible for any one religion to give the correct name to the supreme being. From the perspective of our inquiry this is an especially relevant detail because Radhakrishnan notes that Max Müller identifies Akbar as "the first who ventured on a comparative study of the religions of the world."[19]

The third Western religion, Christianity, also suffers from serious ethical deficiencies. "It used political power for religious propaganda," charges Radhakrishnan. He offers as example an especially colorful footnote. "The African explorer H. M. Stanley remarked, when he inspected the original maxim gun, 'What a splendid instrument for spreading Christianity and civilization among the savage races of Africa!' " Radhakrishnan is equally offended by Karl Barth's uncompromising, militant theology. "Christendom should advance right into the midst of those religions whatever their names may be, and let come what will, deliver her message of the one God and of His compassion for men forlorn, without yielding by a hairbreadth to their 'daemons'."[20] Nor is he favorably impressed by those Christians who are ready to

27

admit to the divine element in other religions but still maintain that Christianity is supreme.[21]

For Radhakrishnan, the solution lies in adopting the Hindu attitude, which is opposed to proselytism. The different religious perspectives can all contribute to the large synthesis which must have been prefigured from the very beginning as "the generic tradition from which they all have sprung."[22]

Many valuable insights abound in Radhakrishnan's work. Especially valuable, for our study, is his impressive openness to the truths found in the several religions and his irenic spirit which counsels that the great religions become "friendly partners in the supreme task of nourishing the spiritual life of mankind."[23]

The philosophy of comparative religion has an aim at once less grand and more demanding. Less grand because it will not seek to sketch out the pattern of a future religious synthesis but more demanding in that it will strive for detailed precision regarding more technical philosophical concerns. Certainly, it will seek to avoid reductionism. Perhaps the charge of reductionism really does not apply to either Radhakrishnan or Schweitzer but then there are passages in each of their works which come close to suggesting such a solution.

The Coming World Civilization, **Hocking**

Hocking announces in his *envoi,* or preface, that he believes he foresees "an emerging common faith" comprised of the "greater religions of mankind." He first attempts to ascertain whether Christianity is a universal religion. He concludes "that it is on the way to become universal, and that its travail through the western passages of modernity has qualified it, . . . to take a certain leadership in meeting the religious problems of the coming civilization."[24] But it is a leadership to be held in humility, because it, like all the other great religions, is still unfinished and in need of continuing reconception. Moreover, the intention of universality is inherent in all the great religions.

It is important to recognize that the several religions are not advocating hypotheses but, rather, declaring visions that have been verified in personal experiences: "This Way is a way to peace." Because all faiths are grounded in a common ground, they cannot clash and there will always be agreement between true mystics.[25] Here Hocking echoes premises already enunciated by Schweitzer and Radhakrishnan.

But there are significant differences to note. The religions of India generally feature a "spiritual athletism" in which personal effort is required to achieve enlightenment, while in the Christian faith salvation is perceived to be a gift of God's grace. Even more significant, the Eastern religions usually regard the ultimate as beyond personality, i.e., suprapersonal, and merging with the Supreme results in the loss of finite selfhood. Christianity, by contrast, conceives of God as Person, and salvation celebrates the communion of person with Person. Finally, the Indian mystic usually tends to withdraw from worldly affairs while the Christian saint regards the mystical experience as "a phase of an alternation which makes him a revitalized participant in the historic work of the kingdom of God on earth."[26]

These are very important insights for the philosophy of comparative religion and they will find a place in the analysis to follow. Especially noteworthy and valuable for a philosophical investigation is Hocking's honest restraint and sense of balance. He reminds us that these contrasts are relative and subject to qualification. Repeating his earlier theme, he finds the variations on the mystical theme all compatible. They all demand discipline, withdrawal for recollection, the initiation into Being so far as the boundaries of human love permit, and all bring healing—"a gift of recovered sense of proportion, of certitude of will, or re-creation, the restored *pou sto* of aboriginal consciousness."[27] For Hocking, a truly universal religion will blend all genuine mystic insights into a single stream.

But Hocking is not suggesting an uncritical syncretism; indeed, he warns against the dangers of "Indifferentism" and "Relativism." The former says "all ways are equally good" in the desire to bypass serious issues, and the latter says "his religion is good *for him*" and is superficial. He identifies what he calls the "Only Way" approach which avoids these dangers but, of course, runs the risk of dogmatism and intolerance as noted by Radhakrishnan. However, if we realize that an honest devotion to the Only Way involves us in a search for "the truth" which is One, then we will avoid arrogant claims and debilitating conflict with other faith claims. The One Way is already present in all religions. "The

29

several universal religions *are already fused together, so to speak, at the top.* "[28]

The end of religious harmony must not, however, be achieved at the price of a dead, uninspiring homogeneity. Such a fate would be in Hocking's view a "desolating prospect," and "the quest for a world faith must retain, in its care for the whole, a continuing solicitude for its diverse members." Through what Hocking refers to as "consociation," worshipers from differing perspectives can grow in the understanding of the Way.[29]

Each of the religions must move toward maturity with respect to reconceiving their faith in the light of the impact of science. But though this requires "glad and intelligent adoption of *the natural,* " it just as surely demands that we do not surrender *"what is more than nature. "* The impact of scientific method demands "simplicity and a care for stark veracity *beneath the indispensable poetry.* "[30] This insight is especially pertinent to recent philosophical theories relating to the analysis of religious language, which will be carefully reviewed and considered in chapter 2.

Hocking's analysis would appear to come closer to a genuine philosophy of comparative religion than do the earlier ones. We have already noted several of his valuable insights. But it is clear even in his title that he is concerned with the philosophy of culture and not with the religious dimension alone.

The Meeting of East and West, **Northrop**

Northrop begins on an empirical note, observing that ideological conflict characterizes the current world scene. At the heart of this encounter he believes are philosophical and religious value systems.[31]

It is perhaps Northrop's most original contribution that he identifies two components that he believes distinguish Eastern from Western religious-philosophical systems. Unlike Schweitzer's optimism-pessimism dialectic, which clearly is developed from the ethical perspective, Northrop's concern is with epistemology. He contends that Western man has developed a theoretical conception of humanity and nature, which though informed by "empirically and experimentally controlled scientific methods, always affirms more . . . than bare facts by themselves provide."[32]

Western religion, philosophy, and science are only partially based on fact and there is always the theoretical hypothesis.

There are two great corollaries that follow from this. First, all Western knowledge, including religion, must remain unfinished and growing as it is continually subjected to reconstruction in the light of new data. Second, the "logic of verification" means that "no Westerner is ever entitled to be cocksure about that portion of his moral, religious, and social ideals which refers to or derives its justification from unseen, inferred factors not given with immediacy." For Northrop, it is in this " 'adventure of ideas' . . . that . . . the genius, and the glory of the West consist."[33]

Northrop contrasts this theoretic component of the West with the radically different epistemology of the East. "For the genius of the East is that it has discovered a type of knowledge and has concentrated its attention continuously, as the West has not, upon a portion of the nature of things which can be known only by being experienced." Northrop observes that artists are concerned with conveying these immediately experienced items for their own sake, and concludes that it is "appropriate, therefore, . . . to call this pure empirical, positivistic, immediately apprehended *a posteriori* factor in human knowledge *the aesthetic component.* "[34] There are two good examples of this aesthetic component in Eastern culture. First, the ineffable quality of its mysticism is thereby explained when we reflect that all empirical data—sense qualia—must be immediately experienced to be known, whether we speak of the Supreme One or the color blue. The former cannot be known without a mystical experience, and the latter can never be known by a person born blind. Second, the symbols of Chinese calligraphy often have "a directly observed form like that of the immediately seen item of direct experience which it denotes."[35] As examples, the Chinese symbol for man is 人, and the symbol for house is 介. It is Northrop's contention that "the totality of the nature of things which this symbolism denotes throughout almost the entire range of Chinese, and even Oriental knowledge, has this pimarily aesthetic character also." With respect to the first example regarding the ineffable quality of the mystical experience, Northrop suggests another characteristic of aesthetic epistemology that bears on the mystical experience. He notes that within the "aesthetic continuum" there is no distinction between subject and object; it is

31

"a single all-embracing continuity." "Thus with respect to the field portion of his immediately apprehended aesthetic nature, the person is identical with the aesthetic natural object."[36] We will continue this analysis of the peculiar intuitive quality of Chinese calligraphy in our discussion of language in chapter 2.

Northrop is certain that both the theoretic and the aesthetic components are ultimate and elementary; irreducible to one another. The Orient has formulated its thought largely in terms of the aesthetic component, while the Occident has employed the theoretic component and now finds itself "in the state of aesthetical and emotional blankness and starvation." But it is not all one-sided, and Northrop's conclusion is that both approaches are necessary for a balanced world philosophy.[37]

Though Northrop's work, like the others', is clearly in the tradition of philosophy of culture or civilization, it provides us with very original insights bound to be useful in furthering the philosophical analysis of world religions. Our very brief summary did not mention the degree to which he investigates and correlates the other dimensions of world culture, e.g., the scientific and the political, but those areas lie outside the focus of the present inquiry. It should be noted, however, that Northrop gives a detailed summary of the various Eastern religious philosophies which goes beyond the previous studies. The philosophy of comparative religion must be fashioned from such detailed knowledge and not sweeping generalizations.

Introduction to Comparative Philosophy, **Raju**

Raju seems to be the first to employ the term *comparative philosophy,* though he is quite aware of preceding work in East-West studies and expresses his indebtedness to it. He sums up the point we have been trying to make with respect to earlier studies: "At the present stage of the development of comparative philosophy in the world or in the author's own work, it is as yet difficult to present a system of ideas constituting a whole; for comparative philosophy is a very young and recent subject."[38] Proceeding to develop his own approach, Raju explains that his study is concerned strictly with philosophy and not religion. Where reference is made to religion, it will be confined to the philosophy underlying the religion. His analysis will be man-centered and stress reason because he believes that emphasis on the supernatural will undermine confidence in reason.[39]

He contends that merely to compare the different cultures in general and their histories will provide useful data for comparative philosophy but will not *be* comparative philosophy. The distinctive subject matter of comparative philosophy must be limited to the philosophical traditions. The value of the study is that it will provide knowledge of solutions to philosophical and life problems from a variety of perspectives based on different conceptions of what constitutes ultimate value. Raju seems to put his finger on the problem when he notes that "comparison of cultures and comparison of traditions have so far been vague, and too generalized comparisons will not yield very useful results." The starting point for comparative philosophy, he believes, must be Schweitzer's insight of respect for life and the will to live, without which there can be neither life nor ethics. Only this major premise can guide the philosopher in developing a world view of and for human life—a "metaphysics of humanism." The new comparative philosophy will bring us closer to having a true world perspective on philosophy. Of course, the great philosophers of the past propounded world views that they believed were true for the whole world, but they worked within the limitations of their own culture. Now the situation is altered and it is possible to do comparative philosophy which will break down the cultural barriers and "revive the original integral outlook, but in a richer and more articulated form."[40]

He subjects three great philosophic traditions to careful study and reaches the following conclusions. Western philosophy tends to be rational and analytical and is best suited for dealing with empirical phenomena. This is why it tends to be preoccupied with the "outer" world and scientific inquiry. Chinese philosophy begins with man and society and develops a powerful humanism. It exhibits a pragmatic spirit which sometimes becomes impatient with abstract, academic questions. Indian philosophy accords reason second place in the hierarchy of values. Intuition or mystical insight is highest in this tradition, which turns its philosophic gaze inward and seeks to explicate the nature of soul—human and cosmic.[41]

While we must credit Raju with identifying the subject and

proceeding to develop a model of comparative philosophy, it does not seem that he has gone beyond a beginning. Certainly, his critique of the three traditions is more detailed than our brief summary suggests, and he observes where a weakness in one tradition may be complemented and corrected with a stronger view from another, but the philosophy of comparative religion should focus upon problems more relevant to religious philosophy and try to resolve them in the light of developed criteria suggested by data from the several traditions. We shall attempt to do this in chapter 4.

World Religions and World Community, **Slater**

Robert L. Slater was director of the Center for the Study of World Religions at Harvard University when in 1963 he wrote his work as an example of how the scholarly analysis of the great religions can be directed to a single theme for the purpose of helping advance the cause of world community. He admits indebtedness to Hocking and Max Müller, whom he credits with launching the study of comparative religion a century ago. Slater notes that the early, widely held belief that all the great religions are essentially the same has given way to a suspicion that they may really be quite irreconcilable. He identifies and explains this change of mind as a conflict between the model of science as a coherent organization of ideas, e.g., traditional philosophy and systematic theology, and the model of science as the objective quest for understanding based on empirical data, e.g., the natural sciences. As the science of religion develops, it seems to Slater to be more and more influenced by the second model.

It may be the case, however, that the phenomenological method offers a constructive solution because it openly espouses empathy as the key to understanding. Van der Leeuw had identified phenomenology of religion with "the general science of religion"[42] and Slater offers, in support, his explanation that "with sympathetic imagination (empathy) he must try to see the other man's religion from the inside"[43] so that understanding is added to description. Admittedly a difficult task, the science of religion must be developed, or do we choose the alternative of

> a babel of crass assertions, a mere appeal to the brute force of noisy opinions, a sheltering behind private authorities, a contempt for all rules of evidence because in some cases it is hard to apply the rules, a

confusion of tongues without hope of communication, exchange or understanding? It may well be that there are limits to our science. But science within limits is better than none.[44]

Of course, no one scholar is likely to command all the historical, linguistic, and philosophical data, but difficult as the task may be, there is no escape from attempting this comprehensive approach, because universal questions must be answered. Eventually, some kind of team approach will probably be developed, but as a start we can at least help to prepare the agenda.[45]

Slater adopts Cantwell Smith's thesis that the study of religion must not ignore the personal factors such as the prevailing states of mind that influence religious behavior. Slater suggests the phrase "depth religion" to suggest that the proper study of religion will avoid focusing on doctrines or "correct ideas" and be concerned rather with the way believers hold their beliefs and their attitudes regarding their faith. We should be more interested in the "middle distance" between religious ideas and religious conduct. He believes that the "prior poetry of religion and the imaginative expressions of faith" require more serious examination.[46] We will attempt to do this in terms of a theory of existential verification in chapter 4.

Without going into the details of Slater's investigation of the several world religions, we can note his conclusion that "while there is small prospect of one world religion there is yet fair prospect of effective religious contribution to world community." The prevailing theme among these religions appears to Slater to be that they are "*tolerantly* confessional." He adopts Hocking's notion of "reconception" as the most promising approach—neither displacement nor synthesis but a rediscovery in each religion of what is most essential.[47] It may well be that the model of religious pluralism developed in North America is the model for future world community. Diversity may after all be essential for the highest order of world civilization.

Problems of Suffering in the Religions of the World, Bowker

John Bowker offers a second example of the application of the study of comparative religion to a single theme. In this instance, it is the problem of suffering. It is this single-minded focus that in our judgment keeps it, along with Slater's essay, from qualifying as a complete philosophy of comparative religion. His analysis concludes with what might have been a starting point for such a philosophy and what must be our starting point when he observes:

> For all religions, there remains the unremitting question of their credibility—that is, of the credibility of their account of existence and of human nature. Fundamentally, this is a question of truth, but it is posed, in practice, as a question of coherence. It is a question of the extent to which religious accounts are, or are not, coherent with each other, and whether they are coherent with other ways (as, for example, the scientific) of observing the universe and of living within it. The exploration of the principle of coherence is perhaps the most urgent task in the attempt to understand the relationship, not simply between religions themselves, but also between religious and secular accounts of existence.[48]

There is no quarreling with Bowker's choice of coherence as the criterion of truth, but his language regarding the logical laws seems likely to cause confusion in the minds of some readers when he explains that

> Jain philosophy is not dominated by the logical rule of the excluded middle, either y or not-y. On the contrary, Jainism (and much other Indian philosophy) values the more subtle refinement of "the rule of manysidedness" *(anekantavada),* which is not congenial to dualism. It is related to the theory of *syadvada,* conditional prediction, which asserts that whatever "reality" may be in itself, it is known by its expression of itself in multiple forms.[49]

Our objection is not with the body of the assertion, which correctly recognizes that a thing may be perceived from a number of perspectives—let us call this perspectivism—but with the initial statement that appears to contrast perspectivism with the principles of identity, noncontradiction, and excluded middle (the "trinity" of logical laws). It is not at all unusual for Western students of Eastern philosophy, particularly beginners, to assume that while Western philosophy is hidebound by the inflexible logical laws, Eastern philosophy is quite refreshingly free of such constraint, or in Bowker's phrase, "not dominated by the role of the excluded middle." This is just not so and we must scotch this misunderstanding at the very beginning of our inquiry. *All* systems of thought, Eastern and Western, must be conceived and expressed in terms of the logical laws. Moreover, any possible thought whatever, no matter how fantastic—past, present, or future—must be developed within those logical parameters. This assertion may be quickly put to the test by simply repeating the phrase "the principle of identity (or any one or all of the logical laws) is false!" Intuition will probably suffice here, but if not, rational analysis makes it clear that in order to deny the principle, it must first be assumed, for the denial itself is what it is and not its negation.

This point has been belabored because there has been and continues to be a great deal of sentimental and fuzzy thinking about religious questions and particularly about Eastern religious philosophy. Let us not be led by poetic expressions and allusions to ineffable mystical states to conclude that we have come upon philosophical-religious systems that operate outside the bounds of reason. Nor is this a simple-minded denial of the nonrational dimensions of our experience; for we are all aware of the richness and depth of experiences of beauty and love and also dread of the demonic. We simply note that whatever the experience be (ineffable or otherwise), it is recognized because it possesses its own identity. Furthermore, any attempt to reflect upon the experience, and later to articulate it to another, must draw upon symbols—mental, verbal, or visual—which must always possess their own identity. Certainly, the beauty and mystery of the nonrational will remain as a major part of the content of our human experiences, but if we ever desire to think and speak about these experiences, it must be within the rational framework of the logical laws. No other course is possible for the intellect—East or West.

An interesting innovation of this study is the inclusion of Marxism, which is perceived to function for many people as a religion. A notable and puzzling omission is Bowker's decision not to discuss the Suffering Servant passages, especially Isaiah 53, with reference to Jesus' interpretation of suffering. This passage is discussed but only with reference to ancient Israel.[50]

Truth and Dialogue in World Religions, **Editor John Hick**

This work is a product of a conference on the philosophy of religion held in 1970 under the auspices of the department of theology at the University of Birmingham. The theme was the problem of truth in the light of apparently conflicting truth claims of the several world religions. A number of scholars express their views on this problem. R. C. Zaehner suggests that in religious discourse, "truth" means that which corresponds to the deepest instincts of mankind and that in the course of development, religions discard what appears no longer relevant and retain what seems permanently relevant. Religions also borrow from one another, and even no longer living religions may have contributed much, e.g., Persian Zoroastrianism to late Judaism and Christianity. In Zaehner's view, the most significant religious development is the emerging synthesis between the prophetic and the mystical types of religion. The Gita and Christianity are bridges between Semitic transcendentalism and Indian immanentalism. This developing synthesis received much impetus from Aurobindo and Teilhard de Chardin.[51]

Ninian Smart believes that lack of clarity about theology, philosophy, and the scientific study of religion has caused much imprecision concerning criteria of religious truth.[52] Santosh Chandra Sengupta seems to corroborate this as he proceeds to demonstrate how imperfectly Hinduism has been understood in the West. He focuses upon the failure to recognize the developing theme in Hinduism from the Vedas through the Upanishads and the Gita to the great Hindu scholastics. He cites abundant evidence to support his claim that there is a "transition from stress on the metaphysical attributes of God to a stress on love as the essence of God via emphasis on His moral attributes."[53] To identify Hinduism exclusively with Advaita Vedanta is to distort the case. More attention should be directed to Ramanuja's characterization of God as Paramapurusha (the Supreme Person), in which moral qualities, especially love, are of paramount importance. Sengupta asserts that God is love *(Karuna),* and "it is an act of loving that is the motive for the creation of the world. Love is not a mere emotion but is the supreme value—goodness."[54] He enumerates Ramanuja's five categories of love, viz.: (1) *Santa* (peaceful love), (2) *Dasya* (servant of God), (3) *Sakhya* (friendship with God), (4) *Vatsalya* (filial love), (5) *Madhurya* (love of God as lover). These insights have been noted in some detail because they might come as refreshing insights to students of Indian thought and perhaps even suggest new ways of solving some special problems relevant to the philosophy of comparative religion.

Perhaps the most significant portion of this anthology is found in

John Hick's response to Wilfred Cantwell Smith's thesis which champions what Smith calls a "personalist level of truth."[55] Smith's thesis was received favorably by Slater as we reported in an earlier summary. But Hick is not so sure and begins his rebuttal by defining the "conflicting truth claims problem" in terms of the different and incompatible things the various religions are saying about ultimate reality, the modes of divine activity, and the nature and destiny of man. The disagreement arises because Smith argues that this is a false problem resting on the false major premise that there is such a thing as "a religion." Correctly perceived, a religion is a human phenomenon that is part of the wider human culture, and one should no more refer to a religion as being "true" or "false" than one should refer to a civilization as being "true" or "false."[56] Smith continues that we must distinguish between religious traditions and the personal faith of men and women. The locus of religious truth is in the latter. For example, Christianity is not "true" in some absolute, impersonal, static sense but becomes true as persons appropriate it and believe it. This is what Smith means by the "personalistic sense of truth."

Hick's response is that Smith's thesis fails to "get us off the hook" of the problem of conflicting truth claims and that he is guilty of promoting "an unnecessary and confusing divorce between personalistic and propositional truth." Surely the various religions can only *become* true in a personalistic sense because they are already true in another, more universal and objective though less existential sense."[57] Hick reminds us that from the extreme personalistic and subjective perspective advocated by Smith, faith in astrology, witchcraft, and Nazism are all "true" because some people sincerely believe in them. This writer most certainly agrees with Hick when he asserts: "To say that whatever is sincerely believed and practised is, by definition, true, would be the end of all critical discrimination, both intellectual and moral."[58]

The solution suggested by Hick is to make a distinction between the various forms of religious experience which characterize the divine-human encounter and the theological doctrines and philosophical interpretations which attempt to conceptualize their meaning. Admittedly, the two components are closely related and influence each other. He then suggests that it is reasonable to entertain the hypothesis that the great religions really are in contact with the same ultimate reality but that largely isolated cultures with different thought forms produced differentiation and even conflicting interpretation in the course of centuries of evolution. The exciting new fact is that modern means of communication and transportation contribute to a radically new intellectual climate featuring interfaith dialogue, which may well result in a converging course for the future development of religion. "The future I am thinking of is accordingly one in which what we now call different religions will constitute the past history of different emphases and variations within something that it need not be too misleading to call a single world religion."[59]

Hick suggests that Aurobindo's "logic of the Infinite" points the way forward because it holds that "different phenomenological characteristics are not mutually exclusive." As an example of how this technique might be applied, Hick examines the apparently conflicting views of Christians and Hindus with respect to human destiny and concludes that "immortality" and "reincarnation" might very well be reconciled in terms of *where* the "continued responsible life" is to take place.[60] This is especially instructive since our inquiry will also endeavor to explore special topics in the context of interfaith views. With respect to "personalistic" and "objective" truth we shall have more to say in chapters 2 and 4.

The nine approaches which have been reviewed in some detail probably constitute the best examples of attempts to view the religious philosophies of mankind critically and comprehensively. Four additional studies will not be dealt with in such detail because one is an anthology and three are analyses from the sociological or anthropological perspectives, which fall outside the scope of a philosophy of comparative religion. However, because they do represent serious attempts to understand and evaluate problems associated with the subject of our analysis, they will be included, briefly, in this section on background material.

The purpose of the East-West Philosophers Conference at the University of Hawaii in 1939 was, in Professor Moore's words, "to determine the possibility of a world philosophy through a synthesis of the ideas and ideals of East and West."[61] To this end, a number of distinguished scholars, including Wing-tsit Chan, D. T. Suzuki, W. E. Hocking, and F. S. C. Northrop, contributed explications and interpretations of the several world systems from their own perspectives. Moore comments that many false and inadequate understandings were corrected as a result of this interchange, and he regards it as a unique chapter in the history of comparative philosophy. That his judgment was correct is borne out by the fact that several of these insights are continued and further developed in subsequent works by Hocking, Northrop, and others who were influenced by the results of the conference.

In what appears to be a cultural or anthropological approach, Mircea Eliade, doubting the value of beginning with a definition of religion, chooses to examine various "hierophanes," or sacred happenings, as they are found in various cultures. His aim is to avoid hypothesizing and try to see "just what things are religious in nature and what those things reveal."[62] His selected data include traditions pertaining to the sky and sky gods, sun and sun worship, agriculture and fertility cults, and the myth of eternal renewal. Valuable insights are shared with respect to the nature and meaning of myths and symbols, but it is not the purpose of his work to make philosophical judgments about the truth value of the various religious claims.

Joseph Campbell's work is similarly anthropological in tone and method but also includes some valuable philosophical observations. Concerning "shared myths," the Indian version of the myth of the One that becomes two pictures the original Self dividing into the first man and woman who couple to produce creation. The Western version is developed in the second chapter of Genesis in terms of Adam giving up his rib, which becomes Eve. These two then become the protoparents of the human race. Perhaps even more significant from the philosophical perspective is his contrast of two views of the ego. The East seeks "extinction of the infantile ego altogether," while the West emphasizes "the responsibility of coming intelligently . . . to some sort of relationship with . . . the Absolute."[63]

The last and most recent work is Michael Pye's *Comparative Religion*. He is very critical of the traditional approach in comparative religion, which presents "rapid and unconnected surveys of beliefs and practices of a few prominent religions" for the purpose of making "discriminating value judgments." He is also critical of the phenomenological method, which to him seems to be grounded in the general assumption "that somehow behind

41

the variety of theologies and symbols, rituals and observances, behind the 'manifestation,' there waits a deeper meaning or structure, a constantly available 'essence.' '' Pye dismisses this as a dogmatic Hindu position and therefore ineligible to be a methodological assumption since a proper method will be free of any theological presupposition. He proposes a new approach to the study of comparative religion which will employ "operational definitions of religion."[64] The data he assembles fall into such categories as religious action, religious groups, religious states of mind, religious concepts, religious and social and psychological factors. These strange *pericopes*—sometimes mere fragments and all unconnected—are introduced by numerical headings reminescent of Wittgenstein's *Tractatus.*

Another very important source not included in our survey is Dr. Peter A. Bertocci's book *The Person God Is.* His approach to the philosophy of religion includes a section that in its critical, in-depth analysis provides us an excellent example of doing philosophy of comparative religion. Because his volume does not develop this approach throughout, we do not include it here, but because of the relevance of his discussion concerning the nature of God from the perspective of comparative philosophy, we will give critical attention to his contribution in chapter 6.

Our original question asking whether we already have examples of the philosophy of comparative religion must receive a qualified answer. A beginning has been made incorporating many valuable insights pertinent to a philosophical study of world religions, but we really have no clear-cut example of a systematic and comprehensively coherent philosophy of comparative religion as such. Specifically, the essentials that need to be developed include the following: a balanced and, as far as possible, an objective overall approach to the several selected traditions, a set of categories to isolate identifiable philosophic and religious interests with rules and criteria for interpreting language and evaluating truth claims, a normative model for guiding an investigation of significant issues and, finally, examples of doing this kind of analysis by focusing on philosophical and religious problems unique to the philosophy of comparative religion.

Chapter Two:
Identifying Categories of Philosophical and Theological Analysis

Categories of Explication

The Philosopher's Perspective

The philosophy of comparative religion will employ many of the same categories as conventional philosophy. For example, the traditional triad of epistemology, metaphysics, and axiology will provide a useful frame for guiding our questions about religion in worldwide perspective. With respect to the first area, epistemology, it will probably be necessary to loosen conventional Western thinking somewhat and give more serious attention to the faculty of intuition as an important source of knowledge while remaining just as critical about the other sources, viz., authority, reason, and experience. We have already noted from our survey of previous work in the area that Eastern thought is rich in language that suggests insight and illumination which we may attribute to intuition. It may be that Western philosophical rigor has blinded us to some of the deeper insights that only intuition can provide. In the same vein, the possibility of epistemic monism should be kept open or we run the risk of prejudging the mystic's claim without giving it fair trial. On the other side of the coin, let it be said straightaway that misplaced tolerance or sentimentality must not dull our use of critical reason. We shall return to this matter when we consider the category of verification.

Turning to the area of axiology, we will need to place far greater emphasis upon ethics and aesthetics than is true in conventional philosophy of religion. While some approaches to the philosophy of religion have recognized the intimate relationship between the moral and the religious dimensions of experience and have developed interesting theories about the moral nature of God and human finite freedom as a prerequisite for the moral life, most Western philosophers have all but ignored the significance of aesthetic phenomena for the religious experience. There have been exceptions to this, and the philosophy of comparative religion must expand these beginnings if it is going to be responsible in its consideration of the aesthetic theme, which we have seen is so predominant in some Eastern philosophy.[1]

The area of metaphysics will be of major importance in this study. Most contemporary philosophers have recovered from the premature announcement that metaphysics is irrelevant because it finds expression in noncognitive propositions. Everyone now recognizes that the verification principle itself is beyond verification and represents a kind of metaphysical utterance. About propositions, noncognitive and otherwise, we shall have more to say presently. Metaphysics must remain an important category of explication because each of the great religions makes some claim about the nature of ultimate reality. Some existentialists and those theologians who draw upon their insights prefer the term *ontology* to *metaphysics* because, as Tillich says, *metaphysics* suggests another world behind this one, while *ontology* deals with the question about the nature of being itself in a more unambiguous manner. Let us keep our options open at this point and let the conclusions follow later on from whatever data we discover. The philosophy of comparative religion, then, will endeavor to explicate the data and insights of the world religions in terms of the traditional philosophical categories but with the kinds of modifications we have suggested.

The Theologian's Perspective

We noted earlier that there is often a sharp difference between the ways theologians and philosophers view religious problems and that these two disciplines might supplement one another to mutual advantage. Tillich has suggested one such merging in his method of correlation in which philosophy poses the questions and theology gives answers. But we suggest another approach, namely, that both the philosopher and the theologian have valuable ways of asking questions about the religious dimension of life and both can contribute to our understanding by their answers. The philosopher who cultivates an attitude of dispassionate objectivity and employs rational analysis in his search for truth is a kind of intellectual policeman who will safeguard our inquiry from logical fallacies and charges of partisanship. But equally important is the theologian who stands within the circle of faith, for in the subjectivity of his faith commitment he may discover exactly the kind of religious data that is necessary if our study is to be empirical, that is experience-based and not merely theoretical data. Therefore, the kinds of questions and concerns religious persons have, constitute categories of explication of the greatest importance for the philosophy of comparative religion.

We suggest the following triad of religious categories, viz., concerns about self-identity and origin; alienation and suffering; and meaning and destiny. It will be noted that this seems to mark a departure from traditional theological categories usually identified as doctrines of God, man, sin and evil, salvation, holy community, etc. The choice is, of course, deliberate because of the ecumenical nature of the inquiry. Terms like *God* and *sin* are simply not universally applicable, while the terms we have suggested do seem to be appropriate in the broadest religious sense. Humanity's existential predicament amidst life's mysterious forces are represented by them.

Take the first theme concerning self-identity and origin and rephrase it as Who am I? and Where do I come from? Even a cursory survey of background studies has shown that every tradition recognizes that these questions are eternally important. The challenge of our present inquiry is to go beyond the almost pat answers of traditional theology and even philosophy of religion and give attention to the quite different answers afforded by Eastern

45

religions and then, going beyond comparative religion, suggest ways to evaluate these claims and insights.

The second category develops questions that spring from the great crises of life. As we have seen in Bowker's analysis, the problem of suffering seems to constitute the starting point for every religion. Traditional Western studies usually include a history of theodicy beginning with the poetry of Job and finishing with the radical view of the finitists. Tillich prefers to see the problem in terms of various kinds of alienation, which include man's alienations from his true self, his neighbors, nature, and Being itself. It is this alienation that produces despair and a sense of meaninglessness. Perhaps Tillich has opened the way to our hearing the problem resolved from non-Western perspectives.

The third category develops questions and answers concerned with the meaning of life, history, and even the existence of the universe itself. Why is there anything rather than nothing? is the question of questions according to Heidegger. Questions about destiny—personal and collective—follow, and various kinds of teleologies are offered by the several religions. Material from the philosophy of history and the eschatological speculations of theology as well as Eastern answers will enrich the content of the philosophy of comparative religion.

Categories of Clarification

Linguistic analysis

Strictly speaking there is only one such category and it is language. It is one of the great contributions of analytic philosophy that it has focused the spotlight of critical philosophical inquiry upon the language used by people engaged in various sorts of discourse. It is a matter of history now that the original members of the *Wiener Kreis* (the Vienna Circle) followed the lead of Ludwig Wittgenstein's *Tractatus Logico-Philosophicus* and developed the famous principle of verification and the concept of logical language. Later, the English philosopher A. J. Ayer challenged conventional thinking about religion with his assertion that all religious language is noncognitive nonsense because, like all metaphysical assertions, it is beyond verification or falsification by any natural method. It was Wittgenstein himself who perceived the limitations of his own insight and in his *Philosophical Investigations* he proposed the theory of "language games," which allows for other kinds of discourse, including "God-talk," besides that which pertains only to sensory data. With the evolution of logical positivism into analytical philosophy, an exciting new chapter was added to conventional philosophy of religion—the problem of religious language—which was to go far beyond earlier theories.

It may be helpful to review the chief contributions made by some modern philosophers and theologians in this area if we are to employ them in our new approach to religion. The Dutch philosopher Willem Zuurdeeg, quick to seize upon Wittgenstein's "game theory" of languages, suggested that religious language is "convictional" because it springs from our deepest convictions about the nature of reality. As such, it is, of course, incapable of verification by either science or philosophy, but that does not mean it lies beyond the pale of intelligent discourse as Ayer seemed to have implied. But, though the object of such language may be "real" enough to those who use it, Zuurdeeg saw no way to establish its reality in an objective sense, and all believers can do is "witness" and hope to convince skeptics by the way they live.[2] This theory seems to identify religious language as a species of propaganda.

From the circle of German theology, Rudolph Bultmann asserted that in order for modern people to comprehend and believe the kerygma—the message of the New Testament—we must demythologize its language. Bultmann reminds us of the overriding importance of the *Weltanschauung,* or world view, that every person holds, which makes it difficult, if not impossible, for modern man with his scientific world view to comprehend the religious language of first-century man with his mythological perspective. But myths are not to be simply thrown out because their function is not to picture the world objectively but to describe how humanity perceives itself to exist in the world. The myths must be understood not cosmologically but existentially. Bultmann's program of demythologizing, sometimes referred to as the "old hermeneutics" in contrast to the "new hermeneutic," has had a profoundly stimulating effect on theology in the Western world and appears to be a technique equally applicable to all religions.

It was Paul Tillich, another German theologian and one who fled Hitler's Reich, who took Bultmann's concept and developed it into a more detailed program for clarifying the meaning of religious language. Myths, says Tillich, are always necessary in any culture and in all intellectual systems—scientific as well as religious. These myths, in turn, are comprised of symbols, and here is where Tillich finds the key. Religious language is essentially symbolic because the symbols point beyond themselves to indicate our "ultimate concern," which is beyond objectification. To understand religious language we must break the myths and interpret the symbols that structure them. Following Bultmann's suggestion, Tillich uses existential insights in stories of creation, fall, sin, guilt, redemption, and salvation. For our purposes, we note that Tillich does indeed suggest that his method should be applied to religions other than biblical, but it remains only a suggestion, as his major effort is limited to an analysis of Western religion. A task for the philosophy of comparative religion will be to see if it can be applied to the other religions with equal success.

The British philosopher R. M. Hare introduced the concept of the *blik,* which stands for basic insight and key to a person's world view. Though bliks are beyond verification or falsification, as the early positivists pointed out, because they can be challenged and supported by reasonable argument, it is possible to make a convincing case for a particular blik. This is what distinguishes some religious bliks from the insane fixation of a neurotic.

The American philosopher Frederick Ferré surveys this history of recent concepts and agrees that the religious statement "God is on our side" functions neither as an empirical proposition ("The sheriff is on our side") or as a linguistic convention ("The captain of the team is on our side"), since no theist will admit that any data decisively count against his blik and because linguistic propositions are factually empty.[3] Ferré suggests that religious language functions (1) heuristically, i.e., it permits us to express our deepest intuitions regarding the meaning of existence. In this sense it is regulative rather than descriptive; (2) emotionally, i.e., it allows us to express our religious feelings; and (3) conatively, i.e., it expresses our will or intention to live our lives in a particular way and this also includes certain performative functions that literally alter an objective situation (e.g., "I now pronounce you husband and wife").

The New Hermeneutic

Gerhard Ebeling and Ernst Fuchs have been the leaders of the new hermeneutic, which goes beyond Bultmann's hermeneutics and linguistic analysis. Instead of regarding religious language objectively and trying to verify and falsify the propositions, the new hermeneutic suggests that we open ourselves and let the religious message speak to us in and through the language. In order for this to happen, we must go beyond an appreciation of sociohistorical factors and try to grasp the intention of the author and the way in which he used his language. The new hermeneutic stresses the intimate relationship between world view and language, even suggesting that the " 'real world' is to a large extent unconsciously built upon the language habits of the group."[4]

The performative function of language is stressed, and if we are to comprehend the significance of religious language, we must try to understand what it was intended to accomplish. Ebeling refers to *Wortgeschehen,* or "word event," which goes beyond mere talk and is genuine revelation that discloses and actually effects a particular kind of future. Attention is given to the metaphorical, poetic character of religious language, which, strangely enough, does not obscure meaning but clarifies—sometimes dramatically.

The goal of clarifying the meaning of a religious text is, of course, not new, but the new hermeneutic goes beyond translation and considerations of literary-historical criticsm to attempt to revisit and revitalize the original situation in order that the original word may be revoiced.[5] This methodological approach has proved very useful when applied to New Testament literature, and there seems to be no reason why it could not be equally valuable when applied to the literature of the East. It would be especially challenging with respect to trying to appreciate the intention of Chinese authors. We have earlier noted what Northrop called the intuitive character of the Chinese language, and it is to a more careful consideration of this phenomenon that we now turn.

The Aesthetic Character of Chinese Calligraphy

This program for clarifying religious language will be applicable to all religious traditions. But there is one kind of clarification that pertains solely to Chinese religious philosophy because of the unique character of the language. We have previously recognized

Northrop's characterization of Chinese language as "aesthetic" and "intuitive" and must now develop this insight. Fung Yu-Lan is in agreement with the point and explains it in terms of the continental geography of China, which produced an agrarian society. Quite simply, he asserts that farmers live in intimate harmony with the land and get to know the laws of nature intuitively. This he contrasts with the ancient Greeks—island and sea people—who traded, counted, and developed an analytical approach to their world. Similarly, the languages of these two cultures are respectively intuitive and analytic.[6] More precisely, the Chinese language has no alphabet or grammar as we know it. It is pictographic; that is, many of the characters owe their form to a symbolic representation of some phenomenon of nature as it was immediately perceived (intuited) by the farm folk of ancient China. Perception, understanding, and communication occur and find aesthetic expression as opposed to the Western mode which is sharply dualistic and analytic. To view Chinese calligraphy is to be caught up and drawn into the original life play in which the happening and flux of time are immediately intuited. It might be compared to holding a filmstrip of cartoon characters and viewing it in a sweeping way so that the characters appear to be moving. Even so, as our eyes take in Chinese pictographs and move vertically from top to bottom, the characters appear alive and we seem to merge with them and the very ideas they symbolize. Consider the following examples. The name Lao Tzu, the legendary founder of *Tao-Te chia,* means "old boy" or "ancient child." *Lao* is represented by the character 耂. If we relax our rigid Western prejudices, we can perhaps intuit the stick figure of a man with a lame leg, holding a cane. The character 子, or *tzu,* is a stylized representation of a child and is also the honorific title "master." Another intuition will perhaps reveal the delightful meaning of the association of those two terms. Now we have the "ancient boy" who is also the "old master."

Now consider the character for *Yang,* the male principle in *Yin-Yang chia.* It is composed of ☉, sun; 勿, shining; and ⼁, mountain. These are the most ancient cursive symbols, later to be transformed into more stylized brush strokes.[7] The final form for *Yang* is 陽. In one instantaneous aesthetic perception we grasp the idea of the positive, objective, mountain-like masculine

50

presence illuminated by the bright sun. Conversely, *Yin,* the female principle, is sketched by integrating 今, moment; 云, cloud covers; and ⌒, mountain—陰. We here intuit the negation of the positive object by the shadow of the cloud. Fung admits that Chinese language is not so much explicit as it is suggestive.

The point we need to understand is that this aesthetic-intuitive character of Chinese language makes all the difference in terms of our understanding the philosophical and religious ideas of the tradition. Not only must we be sensitive to the mythological and other possible uses of religious language so carefully noted by the language philosophers and theologians, but now in this case, we must be aware of the multitude of subtle meanings that surround each Chinese pictograph and allow for "reading in" and "reading out" of meanings on the part of each translator who tries to put it into a Western language. Fung says there are as many interpretations as there are readers! Clearly, we must qualify that claim or all meaningful study will be to no avail. But, at the least, as we read the translations, we can be cautious and ask the question: Is this the most probable inference to be drawn in this case? Always, we should make allowance for the poet's license to employ hyperbole and understatement.[8] A ready sense of humor might also be very helpful, for as we shall see, Eastern thought often makes its point by pricking our sense of the absurd and the comical. After all, to laugh is to give evidence of "getting the point."

We cannot overestimate the importance of applying linguistic analysis and the new hermeneutic to theology and the philosophy of religion. The application of these concepts helps to liberate us from narrow and unimaginative literal misinterpretations of scripture and prepares us to experience something akin to that which moved the author. But Hocking was correct when he pointed out that the biblical faiths have until the present stood alone as pioneer subjects for this rigorous examination. One of the main features of the present study will be to attempt to apply this powerful tool to the other great religious traditions.

Categories of Verification

The Role of Objective Reason

If the philosophy of comparative religion is to go beyond conventional philosophy of religion and comparative religion, it must face up to the challenge to reach at least tentative conclusions that are believed to be true with respect to religion in global perspective. Tests of truth, or criteria for verification and falsification, must be established. Closely related are questions about the sources of our knowledge of religious phenomena. This usually involves an analysis of the religious experience, and it would be difficult to find a better authority than William James, who has produced a sort of model of religious experience on the basis of a great deal of empirical data (empirical in the sense that James studied a "variety of religious experiences") which include Eastern as well as Western sources. Indeed, from the perspective of our present inquiry, we must be impressed when we realize how far ahead of his time he really was. James was very familiar with the details of Vedanta and Buddhism and had even conducted experiments with drug-induced experiences.[9] Students of James will be familiar with the four-point description of the mystical experience as (1) ineffable, (2) noetic, (3) transient, and (4) passive. Based as it is on data gathered from all religious traditions, we see no reason not to accept and employ his model in our study. The work of Otto with respect to the *mysterium tremendum* is especially suited to aid in the interpretations of biblical traditions, and we have earlier summarized his comparative study of mysticism East and West. The Jewish mystic Martin Buber offers valuable insights for understanding the mystical phenomena of the East in terms of his model of the "I-Thou encounter."[10]

We identify the religious experience because it surely constitutes the very essence of all religious data. The mystical experience of the *numen* is the raw material from which is fashioned the cultural artifact we call religion. But we are addressing ourselves to the question of truth in matters religious. We begin with the raw material of religious experience and next inquire as to the source or sources of the religious knowledge that is claimed. How are we able to say that because of an experience we now know this or that to be the case? Traditional philosophy of religion gives answer in terms of faith and reason. Faith might be defined as belief and trust in some thing or person that has not been indisputably proved to be worthy of such trust. We might further identify an objective side of faith, which would be the object of belief and could run the gamut from the trivial and commonplace to the Lord of Heaven himself. On the subjective side we find the attitude of trust, loyalty, and dedication, which explains the spirit of self-abandonment and courage to act that typifies the faithing person.[11] Caught in the tension between our limited knowledge and certainty and existential demands to act *now,* we feel driven to choose and act in ways that take us beyond the realm of empirical facts. Faith is this kind of action; it provides us with the courage to thrust out into the unknown.[12]

On the other hand, there is reason informing us about religious truth. Western philosophy of religion has made a detailed analysis of the nature and function of our rational faculties. The sine qua non is, of course, consistency as defined by that trinity of logic, the logical laws: principles of identity, noncontradiction, and excluded middle. Philosophers, Eastern and Western, are not likely to quarrel with these propositions.

We have earlier suggested an experiment that demonstrates that any attempt to deny these laws will immediately reveal that they must be true. Claims that Eastern thought bypasses the canons of the rational mind are based on confusion. "Going beyond the opposites," e.g., the "bamboo is green and the bamboo is not green," no more ignores the logical laws than does Hegel's dialectical logic annihilate Aristotle's disjunctive logic. Hegel and the Zen masters do introduce the very important notion of process and perspective, but even those concepts depend for their clarity upon the principles of logic. They are what they are and not something else!

But mere consistency among ideas must be supplemented by coherence with empirical data if we are to learn anything about the phenomenal world, including religious experiences. Our gain in richness of content, however, is matched by our loss of absolute rational certainty. The sense perceptors that pick up and transmit the signals to our brains are not perfectly reliable, as we all have experienced, and so we must settle for probable, practical certainty whenever we are dealing with the happenings in the space-time world. This will probably always trouble the true believers who possess positive assurance of the truth of their religious insights even though the philosopher suggests that what they have is not rational but psychological certainty.[13]

These are all points made in traditional philosophy of religion. Now in our present inquiry, we need to be sensitive to a new element with respect to sources of knowledge and the religious experience. I refer to the fact that the "encounter" is not so much with "Another" as it is insight into the true nature of one's own self. The method is sometimes called meditation and may follow a relaxed or a very stylized procedure expounded in the several types of Yoga. Will the traditional analysis of faith and reason apply here? If faith is commitment to something not yet proved true, the answer would seem to be no with respect to faith, because the assurance reached in meditation has to do with self-assurance and not trust in Another. If reason is the conscious effort to formulate and validate propositions, again the answer is negative because enlightenment, or *samadhi,* is said to occur only after one has "gone beyond" discursive thought. We need to add this new phenomenon to the traditional faith/reason dialectic and probably the most descriptive term to use for it will be insight, or intuition. If the latter term is correct, we are fortunate, because there exists a great amount of philosophical analysis about that subject. One thinks of Bergson's suggestions that intuition is the faculty whereby we become aware of perceptual (as distinct from conceptual) time and are able to perceive the movement and growth of living things. G. E. Moore's critical studies about the intuition of the "good," and his identification of the "naturalistic fallacy" are also very relevant here.

Traditional philosophy of religion considers the relationship of faith and reason and whether one is prior, or superior, to the other. We will add intuition to this problem and consider several alternatives. Augustine provides us with a traditional model in which faith always precedes intellect: "If you cannot understand, believe in order that you may understand." He and Thomas Aquinas maintained that there are unprovable and unimaginable premises that only faith can provide but which are necessary if any intellectual endeavor is to bear fruit, e.g., the logical laws, the triune nature of God, and *creatio ex nihilo.* Reason can now work with these premises and build a rational picture of the universe complete with religious propositions, e.g., that God exists. But only faith can complete this structure because only faith can provide us with a vision of supernature which is our telos—the *extasis theoria.*

A second model that exercises profound influence in neo-ortho-dox theological circles has been provided by Søren Kierkegaard who places exclusive emphasis on faith. Religious—at least Christian—truth is a matter of subjectivity—a realm from which objective reason is forever barred. Only passionate faith can appropriate religious truth, so we are instructed to "crucify the intellect, take the leap of faith and live by virtue of the absurd" if we would be true "knights of faith." No matter that this invites logical and moral contradictions, for we are told that there is a "teleological suspension of the ethical" and that our only duty to God is obedient love. Like Abraham, we are to leave one thing behind (reason) and take with us only the jewel of faith.[14]

A third model, suggested by L. Harold DeWolf, seems better balanced than either of the two we have surveyed. DeWolf rejects Kierkegaards's extreme *fideism* and modifies Augustine's and Aquinas' use of faith and reason. Faith and reason must always accompany each other—with no exceptions allowed. No intellectual concepts can be developed without faith providing certain regulative concepts (or bliks, to use Hare's term), but just as certainly, no article of faith could be expressed or even held in the mind without the aid of intellectual categories. There could be no beginning or ending with faith alone for such X's would be without content. Similarly, it is not possible for the intellect to work alone. DeWolf concludes that faith without reason is at its best, fanaticism and at its worst, insanity.[15]

Now what about the category of intuition or enlightenment with respect to these models? Let us associate intuition with faith, since both terms seem to suggest the getting of knowledge by nonlogical methods. Then, there is no reason why we cannot broaden DeWolf's model to accommodate the new term. Even though we now have another source of religious data, we must still integrate it with our rational faculties if we are to maintain the balance of the mind.

This last phrase suggests we already hold a view of what we regard as the objective state of affairs or the truth. The problem of verification/falsification, or truth-testing, is a major one in the philosophy of religion. Three criteria are usually offered. The test of correspondence requires that we match assertion with "objective state of affairs," but clearly there are two limitations. (1) The principle of verification developed by the logical positivists excludes much relevant religious data, e.g., religious experiences that are beyond scientific measurement; and (2) this test assumes that we already know what we want to know, i.e., the truth about the actual state of affairs. The correspondence test will serve us only as long as we are dealing with relatively simple atomic facts.

The pragmatic test is more interesting because it has to do with what "works" in the lives of persons. The statement that if a religion satisfies, then it is "true," sounds very similar to Wilfred Cantwell Smith's concept of personalistic truth. When C. S. Peirce developed this concept some years ago in his essay "How to Make Our Ideas Clear," he used as illustration the controversy over transubstantiation. In pragmatic fact, it really makes no difference which theory is correct if both Protestant and Catholic experience forgiven and renewed lives after partaking of the sacrament. But this solution lacks something as it really avoids facing the issue as to what is objectively the case with respect to the conflicting truth claims. We must recall and agree with Hick's conclusion that "personalistic truth" must rest upon the more fundamental "objective truth" or we risk the slippery slope of relativism. If we can agree with the proposition that truth is that property of a statement which correctly asserts what is or is not the case with regard to the objective state of affairs, then we cannot regard the pragmatic test as final. The correspondence test fails, as we have seen, because we have only another idea about a state of affairs to which we may compare the truth-claiming idea.

We are led to the third criterion of truth, that of comprehensive coherence, an ancient guide that is usually associated with idealistic philosophy because it involves the compatibility of propositions or ideas. But there would seem to be no good reason why philosophers and scholars with different perspectives could not also gainfully employ this test, since it is the principle of logical consistency and empirical coherence of propositions about data that is significant and not the metaphysical presupposition. E. S. Brightman stressed, after self-consistency, that the emerging pattern of ideas should include observation about empirical data as well as speculative hypotheses and that any new truth claim should contribute to the explanatory power of previous assertions. In response to critics who charged that the coherence test was rationalistic, dogmatic, and closed to new insights, he carefully explained that truth claims about the empirical world must be regarded as tentative and only probably certain at best. We must always be alert to new data and new possibilities that might very well necessitate our dismantling large sections of our truth structure in order that it might be rebuilt along patterns more coherent with newly discovered truth.[16] Dr. Peter Bertocci reinforces this spirit of openmindedness by calling the coherence test "growing empirical coherence."[17] There seems to be every good reason for students of the philosohy of comparative religion to adopt, and possible adapt, this truth test.

Elements in Existential Verification

It is to the matter of adaptation that we now turn. Wilfred Cantwell Smith and spokesmen of the new hermeneutic have correctly called our attention to the very important subjective dimension of the religious phenomenon. They seem to have gone almost as far as Kierkegaard, who announced that truth is subjectivity. But our understanding of the significance of the logical laws makes it clear that the claim that "all truth is relative" must be greeted with skepticism. It is a self-refuting claim, because while calling all truth claims relative, it simultaneously claims to announce a universal truth.

However, there is a sense in which the idea of relativity functions quite correctly. Let us equate it with one's perspective or point of view. Truth, particularly religious truth, has a great deal to do with our subjective state of mind—not in the sense that our subjectivity can make anything so but in that our point of view will pass judgment upon the significance of truth claims. Consistency and coherence can verify and falsify, but it will be our state of mind that will cause us to react to it as trivial or as something worthy of our total faith commitment.

Our point of view is a product of our previous experiences, conditioning, circumstances, and choices. Infusing all of this are our moods and attitudes, which give expression to wishes and desires that may be mostly subliminal. Moods seem to be feelings that characterize our mental state, as illustrated by such terms as *uplifted, joyful, expectant, relieved, dejected, hopeless,* and *despairing.* Though these moods ebb and flow in tide-like fashion, usually beyond our conscious control, they exercise a profound influence upon our point of view and, finally, our vision of religious truth.

Attitudes differ from moods in content and in their relation to our will. They are not feeling tones but a state of mind prepared to entertain some specific human experience such as the moral, the aesthetic, the practical, the theoretical, the analytic, or the religious. While it is often difficult, if not impossible, to exchange one mood for another, we find that attitudes are subject to our will. We learn to cultivate the attitude that is appropriate to the situation—an aesthetic attitude at the theater, a religious attitude at worship—though our mood and the encompassing situation will determine our success to a large extent. Together with moods, then, our attitudes help to fashion our point of view, or perspective, from which we will opt for a particular view of religious truth.

Religious truth, it would seem, has a great deal to do with what persons believe to be relevant as well as, perhaps even more than, what is comprehensively coherent. In developing our present inquiry in the philosophy of comparative religion, we must try to do justice to the great variety of perspectives about what is believed to be true. This means that without sacrificing the rigor demanded by the logical laws in terms of consistency, we must seek for an overall and in-depth coherence that includes the moods and attitudes that to such a large extent account for personal perspective and loyalty to a particular religious model of the truth. Some theologians, generally those in the neo-orthodox tradition stemming from Kierkegaard, have developed this subjective dimension and often in a way that upsets the balance between faith and reason, but traditional philosophy of religion generally has neglected it. Our wider inquiry will include such a variety of subjective attitudes that we must incorporate existential elements in the verification process in addition to the more traditional criteria of truth discussed in the previous section. In fact, this may very well turn out to be one of the distinguishing features of the philosophy of comparative religion.

This recognition of the broad spectrum of perspectives on religious truth raises questions about the possibility of arriving at the most comprehensive model of world religion by employing syncretism. If we begin by admitting that there is some truth in each of the world religions, then why isn't it reasonable to conclude that all we need do is put the several pieces of partial truth together to get a system that is most true? This approach has been criticized on two counts: first, it is arbitrary; and second, it is artificial. It is arbitrary because the model would be constructed by a person holding a particular point of view that would be invalid or irrelevant to persons from another tradition, and it is artificial because it would not be a product of natural, historical process and therefore would not be socially viable. But philosophers of religion are concerned with formulating, clarifying, and evaluating religious truth claims. To be concerned with their origins unduly would bring them perilously close to committing the primitivistic fallacy. All oracles and religious pronouncements the world over spring from concern about the truth, whether it be practical or theoretical, and their linguistic elaboration in the course of cultural evolution is not the most relevant factor. Moreover, we are becoming increasingly aware of our ability to consciously shape emerging patterns of culture. If this is possible in the dimension of our religious life, as it is in the areas of technology and social engineering, then the charge of artificiality may be considered to have been met. The charge of arbitrariness appears to be more serious, and we shall attempt to answer it by taking a closer look at different types of syncretism.

We might decide to regard each of the religions as having the same value and develop a kind of equality syncretism that would give an equal voice to each. The balance achieved would reflect the identical emphasis given to each tradition. Clearly, any gain here would be largely political; it would be inappropriate from religious and philosophical perspectives because it fails to recognize the obvious fact that not all religious truth claims are deserving of equal respect. Some claims even appear to be mutually incompatible.

We might develop a democratic syncretism which would give emphasis to a tradition with respect to numbers of adherents. This might appeal to some of those in majority religions but not to anyone sensitive to the logical fallacies of *argumentum ad populum* and *ad baculum.* Majority decisions and quantity of power have no place in logic.

An ethnocentric syncretism would allow the philosopher-theologian to select and weave together insights from the various religions that were compatible with his or her own religious heritage. The resulting system might be consistent and even coherent, but it would not be comprehensively coherent in the strongest sense

59

because the cornerstone would have been arbitrarily chosen without first having been subjected to objective analysis.

Despite the inadequacies of these forms of syncretism, the comprehensive nature of our task requires that we identify and integrate the important truth values inherent in the several religions of our planet if we are to even outline a philosophy of comparative religion. Recall that our investigation of the categories of philosophical analysis has touched on the questions and concerns of philosophers and theologians; special problems of religious language; questions about faith, reason, and intuition; and the human experiences of mood and attitudes. The unidentified necessary subject of all these phenomena is, of course, the person. Let us turn from the artificial and inadequate categories that constitute earlier syncretisms and recognize that the needs and concerns of persons for religious truth constitute the heart of our inquiry. In short, we are suggesting a personalistic syncretism that is, at least in part, based upon the phenomenological approach to the study of religious phenomena.

This existential verification will recognize some of the subjective factors identified by W. C. Smith, R. L. Slater, and those who speak for the new hermeneutic. It will be developed more fully in chapter 4 where we will be concerned with correlating and evaluating the religious data. While recognizing the value of using the phenomenological approach, we remember John Hick's critique of "personalistic truth" and recognize the dangerous possibility of getting frozen into an either/or methodology. We will do well to remember Hocking's phrase "principle of alternation," which suggests that we give due weight to both objective and subjective factors.

Persons are unique centers of self-consciousness and free creativity, whose fleeting moods, interests, and concerns cannot be predicted or coerced and must not be despised. We stifle them at our peril. A personalistic syncretism will recognize this and guide us in reaching conclusions that are relevant to the human condition as well as being empirically true and logically correct.

Now that we have begun to get our categories of analysis in hand, we can turn our attention to selecting data from the various religious traditions of mankind.

Chapter Three:
Selecting Data
from the World's Religions

We have given an account of previous attempts to gain a synoptic overview of the religions of East and West and identified the technical problems and techniques appropriate to our proposed philosophical analysis. Now we turn to gathering the data provided by several religious philosophies. Students of the history of religion and comparative religion know very well that the vast amount of historical, cultural, psychological, doctrinal, and philosophical data could hardly be gathered, codified, and comprehended by one scholar in only one lifetime. But we have set a more modest goal. In developing a philosophy of comparative religion, we will focus only on philosophical and theological features, and in selecting data we shall be guided by the philosophical and religious categories previously identified. In addition to those categories we will make use of some rather traditional but very appropriate terms denoting classic metaphysical orientations. These three metaphysical categories are naturalism, monism, and theism. The reasons for selecting these will become apparent in the course of developing the analysis.

The religious traditions from which we will select the data will be representative of the widest possible spectrum of religious concepts, that is, we will endeavor to obtain a truly global perspective. In addition to the rich tradition of Western theism which constitutes the core and even the details of conventional philosophy of religion, we will examine the traditions rooted in the cultures of India, China, and Japan. These last, as we have noted, are included in conventional comparative religion but not generally subjected to the same intensive philosophical scrutiny so characteristically applied to the biblical traditions. Specifically, with regard to India, we will focus our attention upon Jainism, Sankhya, Yoga, Brahmanism, and Buddhism. From China, Chinese Buddhism and Tao Hsueh (including Yin Yang, Taoism, and Confucianism). Zen Buddhism as developed and expressed in Japan will also be included. Other traditions may be recognized and touched upon as the study seems to warrant, but the traditions above noted will provide most of our data.

Some will ask why the religions of Africa, Australia, and the Americas are not included. The answer is that while a study with a more anthropological emphasis should include those religions, our more limited philosophical analysis of religious concepts will be better served by giving attention to the religious philosophies listed above. It may be that others will want to press on and include other traditions. One thinks of the careful scholarly work done concerning African religious concepts by Jahn Janheinz in his book *Muntu* or the great interest in American Indian religion aroused by Carlos Castenada, but for now, that is beyond the scope of the present inquiry.[1]

Let us make a beginning by taking the regulative concept of "cosmic naturalism," cast it like a great fishing net into the sea of religious concepts, draw it in, and examine our catch.

Cosmic Naturalism

The term *naturalism* is given to any philosophical world view grounded in the major premise that nature—the entire space-time continuum—is all there is. Another way of putting this might be to assert that the phenomenal universe is ultimate reality and to deny that there is any kind of transcendental "supernature" above or beyond this world. Modern Western naturalism is a kind of philosophical counterpart to Western science, which provides the methodology and criterion of verification. However, philosophical naturalism does go beyond strict scientific method, verifiable propositions, and empirical data in the works of Henry N. Wieman, Lloyd Morgan, and Samuel Alexander, who introduce such mystical-sounding terms as *Creative Good, Nisus,* and *natural piety.*[2]

When we turn to ancient Eastern naturalism, the mystic-poetic expressions appear sometimes to soar completely beyond the realm of the natural. However, if we make allowance for the aesthetic character of the Chinese language and much Indian explication, which we have earlier noted, it would appear that we are correct in subsuming these particular Eastern traditions under the category of naturalism. The main point is that the traditions to be investigated do not seem to appeal to any separate, ultimate transcendental power to explain the existence and behavior of nature. The natural cosmos structures the parameters of these speculations, however boldly poetic the form of expression may sometimes be.

Naturalism in India

The rich treasure of Indian religious thought traditionally has been divided into orthodox and heterodox systems. The first, a legacy of the Aryans, is idealistic and monistic and will be considered in a subsequent section. The second is attributed by Heinrich Zimmer to more ancient, Dravidian sources.[3] These earliest settlers of that area of the Indus River Valley presently called Pakistan developed a very sophisticated atomic theory of the universe many centuries before the earliest, sixth-century B.C.E. Greek philosophers propounded similar theories.[4] We will identify two systems that meet our definition of naturalism. They are Jainism and the twin philosophy Sankhya/Yoga. Recognizing that Sankhya/Yoga is one of the three pairs of twin systems that constitute the Orthodox Indian philosophy, we shall follow Zimmer's suggestion that these Aryan systems really contain elements of the more ancient, Dravidian naturalism.

Jainism asserts that the entire realm of nature is a cosmic dialectic involving atoms of spirit, *jiva,* and atoms of matter, *ajiva,* or nonspirit,[5] that may be visualized as a cosmic battle in which the atoms of matter seek to capture and envelop the spiritual atoms.

Once united with matter, the souls are caught in the complex web of the cosmic laws, which range from the physical and biological to the sociological, psychological, and moral. This complex of cause and effect constitutes a law of consequences called *karma*. The drama of existence: birth and death, health and sickness, good and evil, love and hate, takes the form of external cycles called *samsara*. *Samsara*, structured by *karma*, brings pain, sorrow, frustration, and death and is ultimately without meaning. The *jiva*, in turn, struggles to throw off the dumb karmic matter which blinds and desensitizes in order to escape *samsara* which is frustrating its thrust toward self-illumination. In mythic symbolism, the universe is pictured as an immense Cosmic Person (sometimes male, sometimes female), with the lower, more material, phenomena of nature and the demonic creatures occupying the legs and hips. The waist, torso, and arms are the realm of our earthly existence; the neck and head are reserved for the exceptional souls, and the very top of the cranium is where the Jaina saints, called Tirthankaras (those who have crossed over the River), abide in perfect peace and tranquility forever free of *karma* and *samsara*.

Yoga also originated in ancient Dravidian times and is ascribed to the legendary Pantanjali. It is, so far as we can tell, the earliest attempt to employ psychological self-analysis for the purpose of transcending life's frustrations. Some form of Yoga is employed in all expressions of Indian religious philosophy. Indeed, we will see that the influence of Yoga reaches far beyond the Indian homeland. The Jaina saints and all those who desire liberation from *samsara* employ some form of the yogic discipline. The name *Yoga* suggests becoming yoked or linked with Truth.[6]

Briefly, it is a threefold system that includes cultivation of the moral life, physical conditioning, and meditation. Part one, called *karma*, or *dharma yoga*, takes the form of an ethical decalogue similar in outline to the biblical codes. One of the most significant commandments enjoins us to practice *ahimsa*, that is, to refrain from causing injury to any sentiate being. In later interpretations *ahimsa* is given a positive connotation and is understood to mean love for all persons and creatures throughout the universe. The earliest idea concerning this concept must, however, be understood in the light of a different motive, namely, to escape from the interconnectivity of things and events and especially the consequences that follow from being involved in the world. That is to say, *ahimsa,* in its earliest form, probably emerged as the result of the practical realization that causing injury to another invites retaliation and subsequent suffering. If one desires to be free of suffering, then one will practice *ahimsa.* This interpretation is quite compatible with the egoistic hedonism that comprises the ethics of the materialistic Dravidian philosophy called Charvaka.[7] This phase of Yoga may also incorporate devotional exercises of personal piety called *bhakti yoga.*

The second stage, called *hatha yoga,* provides instruction for conditioning the body and achieving physical health. There is a double intention here. First, to be healthy means that one has avoided sickness and gained victory over another kind of "bad *karma.* " Second, only when one has gained mastery over the body (assuming prior achievement of moral living), is one ready to undertake those rigorous mental exercises that alone can lead us to final release from *samsara.*

The third stage, called *jnana* or *raja yoga,* leads us onto the path of meditation. It is a graduated continuum beginning with philosophic thinking about life and the universe, moving into deep contemplation of the structure of reality and, finally, culminating in a mystical, trancelike vision which transcends epistemic dualism, characterized by the subject's observing or contemplating the object, and arrives at epistemic monism, where subject and object are merged and experienced as one. This final state brings *moksha,* liberation from the world, and *samsara,* and brings one to the experience of *nirvana,* that passionless peace which is the goal of all Indian religious philosophy. *Nirvana* has several different interpretations, but here we are concerned with the earliest forms, the first being entirely negative—even nihilistic. The Jaina saints, or Tirthankaras, are completely aloof from the world of nature and its karmic processes. They care nothing for the plight of the suffering multitude of aspiring souls; nor are they even conscious in the personal sense. Their omniscience is computer-like and without compassion. A more positive interpretation is illustrated by one who attains this state and yet continues to live an earthly life, the *jivanmukta.* His only description of the bliss of *nirvana* is the solemn pronouncement "OM." This can be written as the dipthong A-U-M, the three letters symbolizing the three stages of the Yogic path—waking, dreaming, and deep sleep. It is represented by the holy Sanskrit character $3\frac{1}{2}$.

In Sankhya we find an interpretation of nature somewhat similar to the Jain vision, though a different vocabulary is used.[8] Atoms of matter and of spirit are here called *prakrti* and *purusha,* and the dialectical struggle is elaborated to account for the emergence of the cosmos in a quite rational and even believable fashion. *Prakrti* seems to function as the primal "first cause," while *purusha* operates as "final cause" in the evolution of the phenomenal universe. In an interesting and completely unique scenario of evolution, *purusha,* as the natural telos, causes *prakrti* to assume all the patterns found in nature. In the phase of involution, which suggests Aristotle's *entelechia* or the modern DNA concept, *purusha* "informs" *prakrti* of a whole continuum of possibilities beginning with *mahat,* or impersonal mind, and progressing through personal intelligence, personality, sense organs, motor organs, other biological apparatus, and finally to the atoms themselves: earth, air, fire, water, and ether.[9] Now in a kind of reversal of this current, these atoms of *prakrti* proceed under the guidance of the *purusha* to cluster together in all the patterns that empirical observation calls nature, thereby fulfilling the archetypal pattern that inheres in *purusha.* Once the universe has evolved and potentiality has been actualized, the process reverses, and devolution—the destruction or unraveling of the universe—occurs, followed by another evolution of the universe. As in Jainism, the cyclic processes are called *samsara* and recur endlessly.

The Sankhya atomic theory is also naturalistic as no appeal is made to any transcendent power to explain anything. The material atoms of *prakrti* are responsible for their own energy and movement, and the influence of the *purusha* bears a closer similarity to the directive activity of the DNA molecules rather than to divine providence. Sankhya is twined with Yoga in traditional Indian thinking because while the former supplies the cosmic model, the latter is required, as in Jainism, to provide the psychological method for reaching *nirvana.* In both these Indian cosmic naturalisms, the goal is release from the suffering and pointlessness of *samsara* and achievement of the experience of *nirvana,* which is nihilistic in the most extreme sense. Personal self-consciousness and all attendant concerns are permanently snuffed out, that is, until the next time around the cycle.

Humanistic Naturalism in China and Japan

Master Kung, or K'ung Fu Tzu, whose Latin name is Confucius, refused to speculate beyond the empirical data relevant to human society. His humanistic ethic comprised four virtues: *jen* (human-heartedness, or benevolence), *yi* (justice, or righteousness), *li* (propriety, or good manners), and *chih* (wisdom). Three centuries later, Meng Tzu, whose Latin name is Mencius, explained how these four virtues of *Ju chia,* or Confucianism, were grounded in human nature, which is basically and originally good.[10] The feeling of compassion is the origin of benevolence; the feeling of shame is the origin of righteousness; the feeling of consideration for others is the origin of good manners; the feeling of right and wrong is the origin of wisdom. The presence of these four elements in the human being is as natural as the possession of four limbs. The goal is to cultivate the human spirit within and live by the double commandment of *chung-shu.* Never treat others as you yourself would not wish to be treated, but do treat others as you would want others to treat you. The golden rule of *Ju chia* seems to be *chung-yung:* doing ordinary things just right. This naturalism develops the humanistic dimension which continues to be fundamental to Chinese and Japanese thought.

Lao Tzu was an older contemporary of K'ung Fu Tzu and also developed a naturalistic religious philosophy but was more intrigued with the total cosmic frame which supported and structured the human drama. Fung Yu-Lan explains that Taoism, or *Tao-Te chia,* can be analyzed as having three stages.[11] The earliest movement was begun by Yuang Chu and stressed dropping out of corrupt society in order to save one's life. In this first stage, Tao seems to mean nature in a very straightforward, commonsense way. The Chinese pictograph is 道, comprised of two characters, 辶, boat, plus 首, head, and may suggest sailing through life by using one's head or, better, intuition.[12] Our focus is on the second stage developed by Lao Tzu, which attempts to identify and explicate the natural law of the cosmos. This Tao, or Way, causes nature to be as it is. It is the supreme power, and its cyclic process, expressed as "reversal is the Way of Tao," had

67

better be respected if one is to avoid being caught in the undertow and dragged down to destruction. Lao Tzu, wringing out his beard, explains to K'ung's amazed disciples and his would-be rescuers, "I jump into the whirl and come out with the swirl" to safely traverse the rapids and whirlpools of life. He seems to imply that we must let ourselves go, stop fighting the natural forces and learn to ride with them. "The movement of the Tao by contraries proceeds; and weakness marks the course of Tao's mighty deeds" (from *Tao Teh King,* Ch. 40).[13] The golden rule is *wu-wei* : "Doing by nondoing," or "creative quietude." The character for *wu-wei,* 無 為, provides us with another example of the direct, intuitive way the Chinese perceive and express natural phenomena. Notice how *wu,* or "no," is expressed by negating ⺍ by 卌 , and one can almost feel the action *wei,* expressed by the sketch of the person sweeping 為 .

The supreme Tao is not yet perceived to be a transcendental power in Lao Tzu's early thought, as distinguished from the metaphysical speculation so characteristic of the book which bears his name. Fung Yu-Lan hypothesizes that early Chinese thought is devoid of metaphysical categories until it is influenced by Buddhist philosophy in later centuries. These later ideas were then read back into the thought of Lao Tzu in the composition of the book.[14] Thus, the Taoism of Lao Tzu would seem to be a thoroughly naturalistic system. The third stage, which is clearly idealistic, will be considered under the category of spiritual monism.

The manner whereby the Tao produces and sustains the natural order is worked out in great and imaginative detail in the Chinese system called *Yin-Yang chia.* This philosophy also was fashioned in the sixth century B.C.E., but it is difficult to identify any single teacher as founder. Traditionally, the *fang hsih,* or court magicians, are accorded this honor. Several documents spanning three centuries contribute insights to the system; they are the Grand Norm, the Monthly Commands, and the Almanacs.

The cosmology finally developed reminds one of the ancient Indian naturalisms in its essentially dualistic pattern. Only in the Chinese system, we discover a kind of sexual dialectic, with *Yang,* the male principle, interacting with *Yin,* the female principle, to beget six "children" which are rather like the atomic categories of Sankhya. They are Earth, Water, Fire, Wind, Metal, and

Thunder—three "sons" and three "daughters." These "elements" also are eternally in dialectical relationship which produce the universe and all the phenomena of nature.

Yin-Yang chia provides a very elaborate system for computing precise relationships based on characters called trigrams and later, hexagrams. Three unbroken lines, ☰, represent *Yang,* or heaven, and three broken lines, ☷, represent *Yin,* or earth. All phenomena in the space-time continuum can be represented by some combination of these lines, and the entire cosmos is regarded as subject to a single system of causal law, or Tao, which accounts for the eternal rhythm of the Yin-Yang dialectic.[15] Elaborate tables are available for the trained analyst who is able to compute not only past and present relationships in the cosmos but also predict future patterns and thereby give advice regarding auspicious seasons for particular activities. This aspect of *Yin-Yang chia* closely resembles modern Western naturalism in its premise of naturalistic or scientific determinism, though Jung is probably correct in suggesting that *synchronicity* is a more appropriate term than *causality*.[16] Either way, interpretation of natural events is in terms of natural process instead of by miracles worked by a transcendent deity.

By the sixth century B.C.E., Buddhism from India had invaded and thoroughly influenced Chinese thought. In time, several schools of Chinese Buddhism emerged, which to a great degree incorporated the metaphysical ideas of the Aryan idealist tradition. It is against this backdrop that Hui-neng arose to denounce metaphysical idealism and assert a naturalism more in keeping with traditional Chinese religious philosophy. The ancient traditions recount that Fifth Patriarch Hung-jen proclaimed a poetry contest to select his successor. Shen-hsiu, the chief disciple, was favored to win, and wrote a brilliant *gatha* :

The Cosmos is a Bodhi Tree [Nature is a systematic representation of the Buddha Mind.]
Each mind a mirror bright [Finite minds only reflect the Truth.]
Carefully polished hour by hour [Constant yogic meditation is required.]
Lest dust on it alight [Ignorance settles on the mind like dust on a mirror.]

(author's translation)

69

Hui-neng, the typical untaught, rustic folk hero, was illiterate and had to dictate his *gatha*. But the stanzas flash forth like the beatitudes of another hero of the common people.

> There is no Bodhi Tree
> Nor mind like mirror bright
> *Pen-lai-wu-i-wu* [In the Beginning was the Void]
> Whereon can the dust alight? (author's interpretation)

All the ingenious and complex intellectual metaphysical apparatus inherited from Indian thought is swept aside with majestic swirls of calligraphy. The natural cosmos is to be accepted as it is—for its own sake and on its own terms; no *deus ex machina* is required or tolerated. There is no primal mind generating nature but only the infinite potential of the void, and our minds are not simply mirrors routinely reflecting some preordained truth. Rather we intuit the truth about life as we perform our daily tasks. Hui-neng became the Sixth Patriarch of Chinese Buddhism and the founder of *Ch'anna,* or *Ch'an Buddhism,* which draws heavily from the Taoist tradition's emphasis on getting in tune with nature and which developed the Chinese Buddhist notion that *nirvana* is not something transcendental but is wholly within the empirical realm of nature. The chief innovation of Ch'an is its insistence upon instantaneous enlightenment obtained through natural meditation about the way of ordinary things. Once grasped, the ineffable insight may not be communicated to another since it is beyond the power of reason and only silence is appropriate.[17]

The Chinese developed the Yoga inherited with the Indian Buddhism into unique linguistic exercises called Koan, which are intended to help seekers attain to the enlightenment of *nirvana,* which in Japanese is called *satori.* These exchanges between master and monks might well be called dialogues of nonsense because of their strange, exotic character and because they seem to be a stream of non sequiturs. In rejecting idealistic metaphysics, Hui-neng also asserted that classic rationalism is deficient and must be replaced by intuitive method. This is why the *Koan* are characterized by "going beyond the opposites"—non-sense answers, shouting, and direct action that may even involve violence![18]

When Ch'an reaches Japan it is called Zen, but it retains the essential features structured in China in that it is still naturalistic and strangely mystical in a practical sort of way—a worldly mysticism. The nonsense *Koan* continue to stress a no-nonsense attitude toward life which delights the Zen mind that has discovered in the sense of humor a powerful tool for understanding practical living and the mysteries of nature. Two typical Zen stories will serve as examples. In the first one, two monks approach a stream and one proceeds to cross it by walking on the water, but the Zen monk is horrified and exclaims: "Come now! That's not the right way to cross a stream. Let's find a shallow place with stones and do it properly!" Zen delights in deflating pretentious behavior. It is down-to-earth, humane, and kindly. Again, the two monks approach a stream where, this time, a beautiful young maiden stands unable to cross. The Zen monk sweeps her up in his arms, carries her across, and puts her down on the other side. Miles later the other monk remonstrates: "You know we are not permitted to touch a woman." To which the Zen monk replies, "What! Are you still carrying her? I put her down miles back!"[19]

Probably the most distinctive feature of Japanese Zen is the remarkable incorporation of aesthetics, specifically *haiku* poetry and *sumiye* painting. Both the seventeen-syllable poems and the "thrifty brush" style of sketching utilize intuitive insight and lightening-like strokes and thrusts to suggest the wonderful in the ordinary. Suzuki observes that suggestibility is the key to Japanese art.[20] This honors the ancient precept of *wu-wei,* or not overdoing. "Don't paint feet on the snake!" instructs the painting master. Like the *Koan, haiku* and *sumiye* painting invite the percipient to participate and complete the creative process. Here is a joyful path to *satori* which, like the *Koan* way, never leaves the natural realm. Indeed, Zen celebrates the glory of the natural. Salvation can be experienced by finding beauty in sand gardens, bonsai trees, flower arranging, making tea, and perhaps even Toyotas!

Spiritual Monisms

Exchanging one regulative concept for another, we now cast the net of monism into the same waters in search of additional data. Unlike cosmic naturalism, the philosophical monisms go beyond the order of empirical nature to find ultimate reality. The term *monism,* of course, indicates that the multiplicity of natural

71

phenomena are finally grounded in One Source, and because these monisms are idealistic in character, that is, they assert that mind and its ideas are the only reality, the adjective *spiritual* seems to be appropriate. The main idea here is that nature is not regarded as self-explanatory. That is why we must seek for an explanation beyond mere description that can only be found in a supernatural, transcendental Spirit.

Monism in India: Brahmaism

In the eighth century B.C.E., the great Aryan philosophy was developed and preserved in those great treatises known as the Upanishads, उपनिषद् . In this process many of the ideas and terms formulated in ancient times by the dark-skinned Dravidians were taken up and reinterpreted by the fair-skinned Aryan invaders. In general, the ancient cosmology with its atomism, eternal cyclic evolution and devolution, the omnipresent, retributive law of *karma,* and the endless reincarnations of *samsara,* were retained along with the introspective psychological system of Yoga.

The great contribution of the Aryan *rishis* was to suggest that the natural cosmos is not self-explanatory but is the eternal expression of a Cosmic Atman, आत्मन् , or Soul, which they called Brahman, ब्रह्मन् . If we identify the root as the Sanskrit *brh,*[21] the basis of our word "breath," which becomes part of the word "prayer" or "to breathe a prayer," we can perhaps understand how as Brahman, it connotes the One who causes us to burst into prayer. But this Brahman is not to be identified with a personal God. Indian theism uses the word "Brahma" and will be discussed in a following section. The philosophy of the Upanishads develops the idea of a Cosmic Spirit that transcends all intellectual categories—including the personal.

This idealistic metaphysics seems to have emerged as the synthesis of a dialectical problem with Brahman, the Sustaining Ground posited by reason as thesis, countered by the antithesis *atman,* the personal inner self experienced by each one of us.[22] The Brahman concept is logically strong because it explains all of reality in terms of a cosmological argument, but it is existentially weak because no one experiences a mere concept. On the other hand, the *atman* concept is strong because it is existentially verified by each one of us but is weak because such verification is limited to our finite and isolated individual experience. The genius of the Aryan thinkers was manifested in synthesizing the two ideas to beget Brahmatman, ब्रह्म् आत्मन्. The inner *atman* of each one of us cannot be denied without instant affirmation and is therefore to be regarded as equally necessary and primal as Brahman; indeed, it can be nothing less than the conscious center, or the Cosmic Atman of Brahman. We can now understand why Yoga, in the new Aryan interpretation, leads not to the nihilistic Dravidian Nirvana but to the ultimate positive kind of self-actualization: identity with the divine Self. The yogi can now exclaim "Aham Brahm asmi" (I am Brahman!) and "Tat tuam asi" (You are Brahman!).[23]

In the beginning there was Existence, One only, without a second. Some say that in the beginning there was non-existence only, and that out of that the universe was born. But how could such a thing be? How could existence be born of non existence? No, my son, in the beginning there was Existence alone—One only without a second. He, the One, thought to Himself: Let Me be many, let Me grow forth. Thus out of Himself He projected the universe; and having projected out of Himself the universe, He entered into every being. All that is has its self in Him alone. Of all things He is the subtle essence. He is the truth. He is the Self. And that Svetaketu, THAT ART THOU. (Chandogya)[24]

In the ninth century C.E., the great Indian philosopher Shankara synthesized the teachings of the Upanishads. The quintessence produced he called Vedanta, the essence of the Vedas, वेद, which culminate in the Upanishads. To emphasize the essential monism of his metaphysics, he incorporates the adjective *Advaita* (negate "divide"), nondual or monistic. Shankara's Advaita Vedanta may represent the most comprehensively coherent metaphysical idealism to be found in all philosophical literature. Only Hegel's absolute idealism, dating from the nineteenth century C.E. in Germany rivals it in scope and detail.[25]

Idealist philosophers regard the principle of noncontradiction as the sine qua non, and Shankara is no exception. Ultimately, reality cannot be what it is and not be what it is at the same time and in the same sense. While our sense perception provides us with a kaleidoscopic vision of a world in just that kind of flux, for the Indian idealists there is only one conclusion: our senses do not show us the real world. The process, space-time realm must be illusion and so Shankara dubs the phenomenal realm *maya,* the Sanskrit root for our words "mask" and "magic." And, in fact, Vedanta asserts that the world of appearance masks the really Real, which is Brahman. When we see trees, mountains, ocean, and fire, we are under the magic-like spell of *maya.* In fact, all phenomena are manifestations of Brahman. It is, in Shankara's imagery, as if one would mistake a rope for a snake. We have mistaken one thing for another. When we believe our own private self, or soul, is real, we are also under *maya*'s spell. We are mistakenly attributing a quality to a phenomenon, that is, we believe the cosmic Atman can be divided into finite souls. As if one were to call a shell on the beach yellow when, in fact, it is white.

Only Brahman is real; the rest is all part of the eternal cosmic play—the Brahma Drama—a kind of divine sport which provides *lila,* or infinite delight, throughout endless ages. There is the majestic interstellar evolution of the sidereal universe, the emergence of life in all its multitudinous species, the rise of intelligence and inventions, the clash of good and evil, beauty and ugliness, divine and demonic forces, culminating in the coming to perfect cosmic consciousness of all sentient beings. In one final ecstatic moment all the saints know what they really are. As if it were a masquerade ball at midnight, all masks are lowered. Only in this case, every actor has the same identity—it is Brahman, the One, which alone writes, directs, and acts every role as well as providing the scenery! Brahman has achieved perfect knowledge of the truth about all possibilities. This is *sat-chit-ananda,* or reading from right to left, blissful cosmic consciousness of true being. Now the play is over; it has served its purpose and nothing remains except for the grand dissolution and collapse of the universe. Back, and down, fragmented into the primal atoms once again in Brahman, only to repeat the majestic drama again—ad infinitum.

Indian Monism: Mahayana Buddhism

Hiriyana maintains that early Buddhism was essentially a folk gospel of ethical teachings for ordinary people trying to cope with everyday life.[26] Only later did the teachings of Prince Gautama Siddhartha Sakyamuni become incorporated into philosophical speculation.[27] It seems that the atomic naturalism of the Dravidian heritage provided the earliest philosophical foil. Perhaps ancient Jainism with its atomistic structure suggested the synthesis. Or is Zimmer correct in suggesting that Buddhism may even be an outgrowth of Jainism?[28] In any case, Hinayana, a grouping of eighteen schools, the best known being Theravada, or "the Ancient School," is naturalistic and nontheistic.[29] The doctrine of the flux, *yat sat tat ksanikam* (all things are as brief as a wink), is its ingenious interpretation of flowing reality. *Samsara* by the second, it seems. However, our concern here is not with Buddhist naturalism but with monistic Buddhism.

It is not surprising that the dominant Brahmaism would next provide significant insights. Mahayana Buddhism combines the ethical teachings of the Buddha with Aryan idealistic metaphysics. As with all spiritual monisms, Cosmic Mind is the ultimate reality that expresses itself as the magnificent Cosmos and all its laws, but now the great Source is the Buddha Mind, Dharmakaya, or Alaya-vijnana.[30] In most respects it resembles Advaita Vedanta with its *samsara* cycles of worldly illusion and the primary goal of *nirvana* for all sentiate creatures. The devout practice a special kind of Yoga which teaches the Fourfold Truth. (1) To exist is to suffer; (2) selfish desiring causes this suffering; (3) there is a way to extinguish desire; (4) it is the Eightfold Path, or Middle Way.[31] The very important Buddhist concept related to this is *anatta,* or *anatman,* the doctrine of no individual self. We suffer because we first of all mistakenly believe that we have a real, independent self which can desire and be frustrated. To realize that there is only One Self—the Cosmic Buddha—who dwells above suffering and that the sense of existential selfhood is really an illusion, caused by our confusing the temporary confluence of environment, body, brain, consciousness, and sense organs with a unified self, will release us from our false anxieties.[32] The Buddha said to Subhuti:

> Consciousness is like things of magic. Conditions are brought together which create the supposition that something exists. But actually there is nothing that can be that can be laid hand upon. . . . When consciousness is born it comes from nowhere, and . . . when it is extinguished it goes nowhere. But though it neither comes nor goes, yet its origin and extinction do jointly exist. (*Mahaprajnaparamita* fasc. 532, ch. 59 [II])[33]

Those who become accomplished in following the Way are saints, or Bodhisattvas, Helpers of the Buddha, whose vocation is to assist all others, human and even subhuman, to attain *nirvana.*[34] These Bodhisattvas, like Buddha himself, have earned *nirvana* but refuse to accept it in order that they, like their Master, might turn back to render assistance to others. Altruism is the key feature of this system along with the ancient concept of *ahimsa,* or noninjury, which as we have seen dates from the earliest times. *Ahimsa* here is to be understood in the positive sense noted earlier and takes the most extreme forms requiring not only strict pacifism of thought, word, and deed toward other persons but the greatest thoughtfulness and consideration with regard to all creatures. One day, according to tradition, a Bodhisattva took compassion on some starving tiger cubs and hurled his body into their grotto that they might feed on him! The final goal is for all beings to find the Buddha Mind within their own minds and thus to return to the Dharmakaya and *nirvana.* This version of spiritual monism, like Vedanta, promises a positive *nirvana* of blissful cosmic consciousness of the One.

Chinese Monism: Chuang-tzu

The form of *Tao-Te chia* identified earlier was the naturalistic version developed by Yang Chu and Lao Tzu. By following nature and its ways, one hoped to avoid anxieties and assorted dangers. Several centuries later, Chuang Tzu and his followers began synthesizing this naturalistic ethic with the increasingly influential idealistic metaphysics of Mahayana Buddhism. The Chinese are a practical people who generally prefer natural explanations in philosophy, but as Dr. Hu Shih observes, even the Chinese could not withstand the onslaught of Indian metaphysics.[35] Chuang Tzu conceived the Tao in idealist terms as being the metaphysical Ground of Nature—"beyond shapes and features." Tao, like Alaya-vijnana and Brahman, is indescribable because, as the Ground of thought, it is beyond thinking.

> Knowledge had rambled northwards to the region of the Dark Water, where he ascended the height of Imperceptible Slope, where it happened that he met Dumb Inaction. Knowledge addressed him, saying, "I wish to ask you some questions:—By what process of thought and anxious consideration do we get to know the Tao? . . .

But Dumb Inaction gave him no reply. Not only did he not answer, but he did not know how to answer.

Knowledge, disappointed by the fruitlessness of his questions, returned to the south of the Bright Water, and ascended the height of the End of Doubt, where he saw Heedless Blurter, to whom he put the same questions, and who replied, "Ah! I know, and will tell you." But while he was about to speak, he forgot what he wanted to say. (from *Kih Pei Yu,* or "Knowledge Rambling in the North")[36]

Moreover, it cannot be defined because it is infinite. It is not another thing, not even the Supreme Thing or Being, because Tao is the Source of all things and beings. Since only things in space-time can, in any meaningful sense, be said to exist, Tao really does not exist! It cannot be defined, does not exist, and is not a thing. As the No-thing, the Great Source of all things, Tao reminds us of the Mahayana concept of *Sunyata,* or emptiness, and the ancient Taoist concept of *wu,* or nonbeing.

The Chinese sage, however, shuns the regimentation of traditional Yoga and employs a more natural way of contemplating Tao. He prefers to practice his calligraphy or sip tea while contemplating the Ultimate Mystery. He will learn to achieve "relative happiness" by "dispersing emotion with reason," but his final goal is to "sit in the center of the Tao" and enjoy the "absolute happiness" of seeing all things in the light of heaven.[37] His yogic contemplation involves "forgetting all distinctions," including physical, intellectual, and moral categories. His aim is to transcend the epistemic dualism of subject and object, which forever condemns one to second-hand knowledge, and merge his very being with the Object of his contemplation. He believes this epistemic monism is the way to avoid all possibility of error about the object of thought because the thinker knows the truth about himself directly without error and he has become the object of his thought. This, of course, sounds exactly like Vedanta except that Tao suggests the infinite potentiality of artistic creation rather than the supremely conscious Spirit of Brahmatman. As in the case of Ch'an or Zen we note the Chinese preference for aesthetic imagery over intellectual concepts so beloved by the Indian rishis. Even so, the suggestion of positive insight remains as the sage progresses from the state of "having-no knowledge" (ignorance) to "having No-knowledge" (a special kind of spiritual knowledge). In his supremely happy mystical state, the sage "chariots on the normality of the universe" and "makes the excursions into the Infinite."[38]

Personalistic Theisms

Naturalism is content with explanations that are really only descriptions of the way nature is perceived to work. Spiritual monism guided by rigorous logic or aesthetic intuition cannot ascribe reality to the ever-changing phenomenal realm and posits a transcendental realm of Spirit, Mind, or Potential. Both views seem to have their weaknesses. The first suffers for want of an adequate ground or cause to reasonably account for an evolving nature that seems to mysteriously emerge without cause. The second is unconvincing to many because by denying reality to physical phenomena and individual persons, it finds no enduring meaning in the agony and ecstacy of personal existential involvement with the world.

Theists believe that there is a way to avoid the weaknesses and gain the best of both worlds. There is, they assert, a transcendental, self-conscious, and purposing power, called God, who is the ultimate reality and cause, or creator, of nature and individual persons which, by virtue of the creative power of God, are also real. Theism, then, is a religious world view that posits a personal God, or θεός, as First Cause rather than a superpersonal Soul or impersonal Void. Because this God is in some sense personal and the finite, created persons are also real and immortal, we will use the phrase "personalistic theism" to identify this model of religious philosophy. This is the last of the nets to be cast into the sea of religion.

Indian Theism

Theism probably began when man, in an attempt to understand and cope with his puzzling environment and precarious existence, projected his own personal creative power on to the forces of Nature. Just as persons are the cause of the activities in society, so supernatural persons, or "gods," could explain natural phenomena. Before their invasion of India, the ancient Aryans in the Caucasoid region at the juncture of Europe and Asia developed an elaborate system of many gods, which we call polytheism. The poems and chants that constitute the early Vedic literature include hymns to Agni, god of fire; Indra, god of war; Varuna, god of justice; and numerous others.

Emerging reflective thought postulates a primal order in the swirl of events based upon the evidence of harmony and coherence in nature. It begins to appear that all is not mad chaos. The primitive polytheism becomes more sophisticated and takes the form of henotheism, wherein the several deities assume their places in a hierarchy of functions and are presided over by the King God. Henotheism, in elevating one god to this superior rank, does not deny the existence of the other deities. In the Vedas we can learn that at one stage of Aryan thought, Prajapati is regarded as Lord over all the other gods.[39]

The notion of coherence is very compelling, however, and the logical conclusion is monotheism. Once man grasps the concept of cosmos, or universe, as opposed to chaos and "multiverse," the logical need for one cause to account for creating, sustaining, and directing the one universe becomes apparent. As Aryan thought developed, the god Brahma, in this case a personal being—not the impersonal Brahman identified earlier—is identified as the One God. The student inquires of Rishi Vagnavalkya, "How many gods are there?" The first answer given is 33,000 and 3,300! But the questioning persists and the gods are reduced in number first to 33, then to 6, 3, 2, and finally to 1½! "Oh," persists the student, "How many gods are there really, oh Vagnavalkya?" The answer comes inevitably: "One!" "What has become of the others?" "Well, they are only the various powers of the One."[40]

The stage is set for the next development in monotheism: hypostatization, or the introduction of personal characteristics within the One. Deities from the Dravidian heritage are incorporated to enrich the Aryan Brahmanism. Shiva, god of the eternal cyclic natural processes, and Vishnu, god of justice and conservation of values, become the second and third modes, along with Brahma, Creator-Ground and first mode, in the Hindu trinity, the Trimurti. This theism is developed in the two great epics the Mahabharata and the Ramayana. In the first epic, the most well-known section, called the Bhagavad-gita, develops the concept of providential care for humans in times of trouble. Here one finds the notion of the *avatar,* or savior, who is an incarnation of the divine.[41] Rama and Krishna are divine saviors, manifestations of Vishnu, who assist humankind in the struggle for justice and ethical self-realization in the face of evil and suffering. Loyal worshipers practice bhakti yoga—the way of faith—to find the meaning of life in the midst of *samsara.* The ethical dimension finds strong expression in the concepts of *dharma* and *karma* : duty and moral and natural laws as developed in the complex appartus of the caste system.

Indian personalistic theism may find its most complete philosophical expression in the thought of Ramanuja who lived in the twelfth century C.E. Ramanuja reacted strongly against Shankara's absolute monistic idealism as expounded in Advaita Vedanta. The notion that the phenomenal realm of nature, including all finite persons, is finally unreal, or *maya,* posed more problems than it solved. Ramanuja argued that since Brahma (he preferred the personal appellation to the impersonal Brahman used by Shankara, and Narayana was Ramanuja's favorite name for God) was absolutely real, everything he created must also be real by virtue of its derivation from him.[42] Therefore, nature and individual persons are not at all illusory but really real. They are the eternally real expressions of the real God. Furthermore, Ramanuja must have had a deep insight into the phenomenon of the interpersonal relationship. He was deeply religious as well as a critical philosopher and felt that Shankara's absolute monism failed to meet our deepest existential, personalistic needs. The One of Advaita seems terribly alone when stripped of all the trappings of the Cosmic Play. Without real persons how could there be any love? Love is the sharing which can only occur between real persons, and without a community of persons, love—with only One Person—would be reduced to a lonely self-love.

> Those who worship Me out of intense love because they cannot sustain their souls without worshiping Me, which worship is their sole aim, whether they are born in a high caste or a low caste, exist within My very self provided with every happiness as though their qualities were equal to Mine. "I, too, am in them" means: I treat them as if they were My superiors. (from *Gitabhasya* 9.29)[43]

Ramanuja opts for personalism because on both rational and existential grounds it answers more questions and meets more of our deepest personal needs than esoteric monism. It is more satisfying and seems more truthful. He called his personalistic theism Vishistadvaita Vedanta, or qualified nondualism. Vishistadvaita also assumes a trinitarian form consisting of three eternal modes: (1) Brahma as metaphysical Ground and Creator; (2) Brahma eternally manifested in nature; (3) Brahma eternally manifested through humanity. The goal is not to escape the illusion of individuality and realize our Cosmic Atman as in Advaita but rather to realize the divine quality and power in each finite person so that, together, we might realize an ideal society on Earth—a brahmaloka, or kingdom of Brahma. [44]

> The finite self *[jivatma]* has Brahman as its Self, for it is His mode *[prakara]* since it is the body *[sarira]* of Brahman. . . . All things having one of the varieties of characteristic physical structure . . . are the modes of finitie individual selves, since they are their respective bodies. This means that these physical objects, too, are ensouled by Brahman. (from *Vedarthasamgraha* 17b-18a) [45]

But on closer examination it seems that Ramanuja's qualified monism is not finally personalistic if personalism asserts the literal ontological reality of individual souls. After all, Ramanuja's point is that the phenomena of nature and persons are eternal modes of the one Brahma. Really, it is Madhva, thirteenth century C.E., who unequivocally insists that differences are real. Specifically, Brahma, or God, is not the natural world nor is he the community of persons. God creates the world by causing the primeval matter of *prakrti* to evolve into a universe that subsequently devolves only to repeat the process eternally. God is thus final cause but not also material cause as Ramanuja insists. Likewise, God creates finite souls who are distinct from him though they are similar in spiritual attributes and potential enjoyments. [46] In this way, Madhva seems to retain the important feature of individual souls as free and responsible centers of creativity. The concept of freedom is vital to the arguments for the moral and intellectual life, but as we shall observe later, there are serious questions to be raised regarding Madhva's view of persons.

Madhva's argument for difference (or dualism), which is the basis for the name Dvaita (divided) Vedanta, is an epistemological one. First, observes Madhva, perception, the basis of all knowledge depends upon realizing differences. Clearly, without differences there could be no perception and no knowledge. Secondly, you cannot deny this without asserting something else to be the case, which involves making a distinction. Such a contradiction invalidates the denial. Hence, it follows that differences are real.[47] Madhva's epistemic dualism is compatible with the truth criterion of comprehensive coherence which can assist us in obtaining rational certainity as contrasted with the psychological certainity that the epistemic monism of monistic metaphysics offers.

In modern Indian thought, Aurobindo has developed this kind of personalistic theism. The ideal society is a community of saints who practice perfect love toward one another and remind us of the model of the Buddhist Bodhisattva. They intuit the truth about the phenomenal realm and are in psychic command of all atomic processes, thereby solving all energy problems and eliminating the need for technology. Their mental control of all metabolic processes will eliminate all kinds of sickness and disease and, finally, even death itself. By means of extrasensory perception they communicate and gain intuitive knowledge of one another. Each one knows himself to be a "poise of being for Brahma." The purpose of cosmic evolution is realized in the emergence of these "gnostic beings" who dwell in the bliss of eternal creative fellowship with the personal Brahma.[48]

> A supramental or gnostic race of beings would not be a race made according to a single type, molded in a single fixed pattern; for the law of the Supermind is unity fulfilled in diversity, and therefore there would be an infinite diversity in the manifestation of the gnostic consciousness.
>
> The gnostic individual would be the consummation of the spiritual man; his whole way of being, thinking, living, acting would be governed by the power of a vast universal spirituality.
>
> An evolution of gnostic consciousness brings with it a transformation of our world-consciousness and world-action. . . . The gnostic being will take up the world of Life and Matter, but he will turn and adapt it to his own truth and purpose of existence; he will mold life itself into his own spiritual image, and this he will be able to do because he has the secret of a spiritual creation and is in communion and oneness with the Creator within him.[49]

Western Theism

The ancient Semitic people of the Middle East were "cousins" of the Aryans who had brought theism to India. The Semitic *habiru,* or "wandering ones," traversed the fertile crescent between the Tigris/Euphrates and the Nile river systems seeking food and water for their flocks and shelter from other marauding desert bands. Like their Aryan cousins, they developed a polytheism around their "El gods." This linguistic form resulted from linking *El,* the supreme god of the Canaanite pantheon, with the various gods of the patriarchal religion, producing such names of *El Shaddai,* god of might or god of the mountains; *El Roi,* god of seeing; *El Bereth,* god of the covenant; and *El Olam,* everlasting god. Abraham's tribe worshiped the Defender; Jacob's tribe, the Mighty One; and Isaac's, the Fearful One. The stories in the book of Genesis, although edited by redactors to express the monotheism of a later age, seem to preserve elements of this ancient polytheism.[50]

The Mosaic period (1300 B.C.E.) introduced henotheism, which may be precisely verified by the First Commandment, "Thou shalt have no *other* gods before [or besides] me" (Exod. 20:3; Deut. 5:7). It is possible that the historic person called Moses may have intended to introduce his unready people to the monotheism he had himself learned during Egyptian schooling in the tradition of Pharaoh Ikhnaton. In any event, Moses had a powerful religious experience and identified the Holy Power with the Midianite god Yahweh, יְהֹוָה —"I AM," or "I will be what I will be."[51] From this time forward, Yahweh is the God of Israel, more powerful than all other gods. He shows his concern and power by delivering his chosen people Israel from their Egyptian captors and promises to lead them into the Promised Land. The Hebrew faith is founded on the rock that God has acted in history to show love toward his people and, therefore, they ought to respond in gratitude and be faithful to him by observing the conditions of the Covenant (*Bereth*— בְּרִית).

In the eighth century B.C.E., there appeared commanding figures, sensitive and articulate, called prophets. Unlike the charismatic "seers" or "sons of the prophets" who were their precursors, these religious geniuses were able to analyze their religious intuitions and articulate them in eloquent poetry called oracles.[52] The first of these was Amos, a shepherd from Tekoa in the south. He was probably the first writing prophet, and his vision of a universal moral law authored and upheld by Yahweh marks the beginning of monotheism in Israel. "I hate, I despise your feasts, and I take no delight in your solemn assemblies. . . . But let justice roll down like water, and righteousness *[mshpat—* מִשְׁפָּט *]* like an everflowing stream" (Amos 5:21-24).

His contemporary Hosea supplemented this foundational insight with the corollary proposition that Yahweh is also a loving God comparable to a husband and father. Perhaps Hosea's own domestic tragedy involving his faithless wife, Gomer, provided the basis for this insight.[53] These two prophets provided the components for the concept that defines God as ethical love. This may well be the most unique and significant contribution of Western theism.

> Therefore, behold, I will allure her, and bring her into the wilderness, and speak tenderly to her. . . . And in that day, says the Lord, you will call me, "My husband" . . . and I will make you lie down in safety. And I will betroth you to me for ever; I will betroth you to me in righteousness and in justice, in steadfast love *[hesed—* חֶסֶד *]*, and in mercy. I will betroth you to me in faithfulness; and you shall know the Lord. (Hos. 2:14-20)

Isaiah of Jerusalem developed the ancient theme of Yahweh as Lord of history. Political events are to be understood in the light of God's purpose which evolves as a *Heilsgeschichte,* or holy history. Yahweh, beyond all description, can only be acknowledged by exclaiming *Kodesh, Kodesh* (holy, holy!), and obedient faithfulness is the only acceptable response to his commands.[54]

The poet-prophet of Israel's exile is sometimes identified as Deutero Isaiah. He pondered the meaning of Israel's suffering for two generations in Babylon and sang the moving poems of the Suffering Servant, which portray the ideal Israel as God's Servant punished for faithless Israel's violation of the Law. Nevertheless, he provides the nations of the world with a marvelous opportunity to inherit the New Age of peace, justice, and prosperity if only they will learn from the Servant. The message is that vicarious suffering can be redemptive. "With his stripes we have been healed!" (Isa. 53). This positive philosophy of the constructive use of suffering seems unparalleled in any nonbiblical world religion.

The sixth century B.C.E. marks a significant turning point in the development of Western theism when the Persian religion Zoroastrianism contributed several significant insights, viz., a Last Battle called Armageddon, in which God (Ahura Mazda) and his angels defeat the devil (Ahriman) and his demons. This is accompanied by an apocalyptic end of the world complete with earthquakes, falling stars, and other miraculous signs. Finally, there is the notion of life after death in heaven or hell after a worldwide physical resurrection and judgment of all the dead. Those Israelites who were exiled to Babylon came in contact with these ideas and incorporated this "apocalyptic hope" into their thinking about a messiah—one annointed by God—who would come from heaven to save Israel from foreign domination and bring peace to earth.[55]

Jesus of Nazareth was a first-century rabbi, who incorporated into his ministry the ethical teachings of the great prophets. Hosea seems to have especially influenced Jesus (both names mean "God saves"), who adopted Hosea's figure of God as loving heavenly Father and made it central to his teaching.

> You have heard that it was said, "You shall love your neighbor and hate your enemy." But I say to you, love your enemies and pray for those who persecute you, so that you may be sons of your Father who is in heaven. (Matt. 5:43-45*a*)

Though both apocalyptic and immanental passages regarding the coming of an age of peace on earth (the kingdom of God) can be found in the Gospels, the latter seem to represent Jesus' mature thought. "The kingdom of God is not coming with signs to be observed; nor will they say, 'Lo, here it is!' or 'There!' for behold, the kingdom of God is within you" (Luke 17:20-21).

That Jesus was more than an effective teacher of religion and ethics is borne out by the fact that he consciously took upon himself the role of Suffering Servant and invested his life in what he believed was God's plan for inaugurating the Kingdom on earth. The drama of Jesus' confrontation with what he believed to be a corrupt establishment, his arrest, conviction, and cruel death, and his followers' belief that his spirit had triumphed and lived among them, became material for a new world religion. These followers of the Way believed that Judaism had found its culmination in Christianity. To this day, serious differences of interpretation concerning apocalypticism and immanentalism continue. Some believe that Jesus will return physically (parousia) on the Last Day, while others suggest that the key is to be found in the Fourth Gospel where paraclete (Comforter) replaces parousia and Christ comes to every believer at the moment of his confession of faith.[56]

Paul of Tarsus probably deserves to be recognized as the first imaginative interpreter of the person and work of Jesus. Often his efforts are termed the "religion about Jesus" in contrast to the "religion of Jesus," but this is only partially correct because the elements selected and given theological expression by Paul were implicit in Jesus' ministry and message.

We refer, of course, to the concepts of salvation by faith and freedom from the law of Jewish Torah proclaimed in Paul's Letter to the Galatians and developed in his Epistle to the Romans. Paul came to the realization that even a sensitive person of good will with the very best of intentions cannot perfectly keep the moral law of Torah. The point had been earlier made by Jesus when he proclaimed that inner dispositions and motives as well as the overt acts count. To reinforce the point, he proclaims: "You, therefore, must be perfect, even as your heavenly Father is perfect" (Matt. 5:48). Not only does autonomous striving for righteousness fail, but it produces frustrations, guilt, and despair. Paul's own experience grounds his dramatic cry: "For I do not do the good I want, but the evil I do not want is what I do. . . . Wretched man that I am! Who will deliver me from this body of death?" (Rom. 7:19-24). And again: "For all those who rely on works of the law are under a curse" (Gal. 3:10). But it is Paul's great insight to see the ministry of Jesus as the "good news" about a gracious God who will accept our sincere intention to live in the Christ Spirit in lieu of actual righteousness. What is required is acceptance of and radical commitment to Jesus Christ as the normative model of perfect humanity and clearest revelation of deity. This new orientation constitutes an act of faith that opens the way for God's grace to work in and through the believer and lead him into the "new life in Christ." Paul says, "We . . . know that a man is not justified [or reckoned righteous] by works of the law but through faith in Jesus Christ" (Gal. 2:15-16). It is now possible to be "justified by his grace as a gift, through the redemption which is in Christ Jesus" (Rom. 3:24).

There is more to Paul's insight than a way of escaping despair. The other side of despair about failure to accomplish is pride over accomplishment. One can hardly overestimate the significance of overweening pride ('υβρις), which has long been identified by theologians as the original sin. It is in Augustine's words self-love *(amor sui)* and results in love of the world *(cupiditas)* over love of God *(amor dei)*. This is "original" sin in the ontological-psychological sense and not, as the biblical literalists suppose, a mere chronological sense. It is pride that triggers every base human desire and act that spells separation from God and human community. But Paul sees that faith dispells pride. "Then what becomes of our boasting? It is excluded. On what principle? On the principle of works? No, but on the principle of faith" (Rom. 3:27).

These notions of freedom from the law and salvation by faith are not intended to be amoral as some of his hearers imagined. To the antinomians he exclaimed: "Do we then overthrow the law by this faith? By no means! On the contrary, we uphold the law" (Rom. 3:31). But the very minutely spelled out ethic of Judaism had been transformed into the ethos of the Christian Way, which is identified by αγάπη, love. Paul exhorts: "Owe no one anything, except to love one another; for he who loves his neighbor has fulfilled the law" (Rom. 13:8). Augustine later reformulated it: "Love God and do as you please!" The people of faith will find it possible to offer this love because it has first been given to them by their God of love. It is, of course, not an automatic transaction. Respect for the dignity of the person requires that they be free to accept or reject God's gift.

Christianity was given intellectual vigor as it interacted with Greek philosophy. Stoicism contributed the idea of Logos, λόγος, the "Creative Wisdom," which is metaphysical ground of all being. John of the Fourth Gospel personalized the Power when he identified Logos with the Christ of the Gospel tradition. Later, in the great church councils of the third and fourth centuries, this insight was expanded by stages producing a trinitarian model of the Godhead. Contrary to much popular misconception, the normative concept is not tritheistic. Unequivocal monotheism is clearly intended as the word translated "person" in modern English is

87

persona in Latin and *prosopon* in Greek. Both terms refer to the theater, specifically to the masks worn by actors. God in three *personae* is God in three dramatic roles all played simultaneously, not successively.

The religious ideas we have selected and viewed in the light of three philosophical metaphysical models constitute the empirical data in our analysis. Now we must review this material in the light of the categories we identified in chapter 2.

Chapter Four:
Truth Testing and
Model Building

We are at a critical point in the development of our analysis. To this point, our task has involved the rather straightforward procedure of reviewing earlier efforts and presenting selected data from the great religions. Now we must see if it is possible to find new insights using the material. This will involve the clarification and evaluation of the data we have assembled. Our aim is to combine critical philosophical analysis with the global perspective of comparative religion and is the reason for trying to construct a philosophy of comparative religion.

A four-step procedure seems to offer the best approach. First, there is the task of sorting out key ideas and correlating them with the categories of explication identified in chapter 2. The major headings will be: metaphysical and cosmological questions, axiological questions, and existential concerns. This categorization will facilitate the second and third steps, which involve the very difficult matter of evaluation. A serious study must give careful attention to the manner in which judgments are made if we are to avoid charges of being dogmatic, prejudiced, or even superficial and trivial. Last, we will attempt to construct a provisional, or working, model of world religion based on our findings. Two points must be made immediately to allay false apprehensions. First, we disclaim any prophetic stance that might suggest our model is intended to prefigure some future state of affairs regarding a world religion on planet Earth. That is not the purpose of our study. Second, the model is intended to be normative, not descriptive, regarding the truth value of major propositions gleaned from the data of world religion. If successful, our model could be used as a kind of regulative design or composition in the light of which a number of problems relating to comparative religion could be checked and evaluated. In fact, this last marks the real beginning of doing the philosophy of comparative religion and will be further developed in part II.

Correlating the Data with the Categories of Explication

Metaphysical and Cosmological Questions

Probably the most unique feature of the several cosmic naturalisms is their way of avoiding the metaphysical question. Whether they are developing a world view in terms of mechanistic atomism, matter-spirit dualism, *samsara* cycle, or sexual dialectic of the natural way, no reason if proffered to explain why anything exists or why it is the way it is. Nature is always regarded as self-explanatory. It is a self-sufficient category and its own *raison d'être*. In fact, for Zen, perhaps the most sophisticated form of naturalism, metaphysical problems are rejected as improper concerns.

But though there is a kind of style or charm about Zen which suggests we stop wasting our time trying to solve problems of our own making and learn to dissolve them instead, to those of a metaphysical turn of mind there seems to be no excuse for this kind of avoidance. The "why" questions still haunt us, and we want an explanation as distinguished from mere description. However, the naturalisms give much attention to cosmological explanation. They provide several models of cosmic evolution and devolution which are highly imaginative and very sophisticated in terms of rational and scientific categories of thinking.

The spiritual monisms, whether Indian Vedanta, Mahayana Buddhism, or Chinese Taoism as interpreted by Chuang Tzu, all attempt to offer serious answers to the metaphysical questions. The absolute idealism of Vedanta seems to be the strongest by virtue of its rigorous logic which rests uncompromisingly upon the very strictest interpretation of the law of noncontradiction when it asserts not both one and non-one, i.e., not both one and many. The reason given for the phenomenal world is interesting and imaginative. It is the way the One (Brahman) passes eternal time and escapes intolerable boredom. "He" finds delight *(lila)*, cosmic play, and sport in the creative activity of cosmos making. Taoism expands upon the aesthetic dimension of this answer. The phenomenal realm is the product of the eternal realization of the primal "Uncarved Block," which is suggestive of the infinite aesthetic potential in the sculptor's block before he begins to create. This metaphysical "Block," though, carves itself without the aid of the artist, and it eternally produces an infinite number of creations. Mahayana Buddhism develops its legacy of Indian metaphysics and posits the Cosmic Buddha Mind, Dharmakaya, as the eternal Ground whose purpose is the continuing realization of compassion and sensitivity in the Bodhisattvas.

The theisms provide answers that reflect more personalistic concerns. The universe is created to serve as a stage for the human historical drama in which interpersonal self-realization is the telos, or goal. Cyclic natural process in Indian thought and holy history in the biblical tradition are the instrumental means whereby God, or Brahma, achieves his will. The Gita suggests that the law of *karma,* or justice, is the guiding factor. In the biblical tradition we note that the prophet Amos is in agreement, but Hosea and Deutero Isaiah and later New Testament literature augment this with the concept of love, first as *hesed,* or loyalty, and gratitude to God and fellow human beings; and later, as *agape,* or unmerited and unmeasured love, poured out by the Father God to his children. In fact, this love theme is used as an explanation for creation when it is pointed out that love by nature wants to share its values and its power with the beloved. God is defined as the loving Father who creates because he is this *agape* love.[1] Clearly, Heidegger's fundamental metaphysical question, Why is there something rather than nothing? finds a powerful answer in biblical theism. Its explanatory power is said to become increasingly apparent as the full range of possibilities inherent in it become recognized.

Theism's cosmological explanations, however, are developed in

91

terms of anthropomorphic language and can lead to serious problems when interpreted literally and correlated with scientific categories of thinking and empirical data. In the most conservative theistic models, the eschatological view is seriously limited with its insistence on only one time and one chance to get into harmony with the divine, followed by disposition to heaven or hell for all eternity. It is especially troublesome in its literal apocalyptic interpretation in terms of ethical as well as scientific and rational categories.

Axiological Questions

Intellectual values are recognized by all the systems with the possible exceptions of Zen and early Taoism. As mentioned before, the idealisms are most aware of the intellectual demand for logical consistency and comprehensive coherence. All intellectual problems are answered in terms of a Cosmic Mind which is the very ground of meaning. Mind is the ground of all values, and the world makes sense in these terms in spite of all the seeming contradictions. Indeed, the whole reason for existence seems to be an intellectual one, i.e., conquest of ignorance, most clearly asserted in the Vedantist exclamation "Aham Brahm asmi" (I know who I am—I am God!).

The naturalisms are certainly rational but only in a restricted sense. The intellectual values they display are not finally grounded in a metaphysical first cause that would explain their values; nor do the theisms make the intellectual values primary. The emphasis on the ontological status of each individual—an existential demand—raises questions about the unitary nature of ultimate reality demanded by reason.

Moral values are recognized in the naturalisms, especially in the Confucianist ethic of Tao Hsueh. Even pessimistic Jainism and Sankhya recognize the fact of *karma* and the need to cultivate the moral virtues. But it is a mechanical, almost computer-like scorekeeping, and there does not seem to be any intrinsic worth attributed to the moral life. In Zen, righteousness seems to mean getting into harmony with nature, as is the case in Chinese Taoism. But Zen seems quite relativistic, and no enduring norms of right and wrong are suggested. The existential situation appears to prescribe the conduct.

The monisms vary in their attention to the problem. Advaita Vedanta places great emphasis on moral achievement. In the decalogue of Yoga, the virtuous life is prescribed, but finally, it appears to be only instrumental for attaining the goal of *moksha* (release from ignorance), which takes precedence over the ethical life. Mahayana calls for ethical living with emphasis on compassion, but justice and social order seem neglected. Taoism moves beyond justice and ethical values when it proclaims that the sage lives a life beyond moral distinctions in which the mystical value takes precedence over all other values.

The theisms put the most emphasis on ethical values. This is, of course, implicit in their personalistic structure in which the I-Thou relationship is absolutely primary. They are first of all personalistic and persons cannot exist in community without moral values and norms. Since theisms define a person, at least in part, as having character, the ethical values must be of intrinsic worth. Moreover, the theisms develop the concept of the ethical in terms of a kind of love that rises above nonrational affection and includes knowledge, respect, concern, and care.[2] The synthesis is called ethical love. True, Confucianism lists *jen* (human-heartedness) as an important ethical value, but it is not finally seen as rationale for creation itself as in the case of biblical theism. The same observation holds for Indian theism, where the closest we might come to finding love at the center is to note Brahma's love for Self. But even so, this kind of self-love finds expression as intellectual curiosity and desire to escape boredom rather than compassion for other persons.

Aesthetic values find a prominent place in the naturalisms, especially in Tao Hsueh and Zen. In the former, the complex yet unified cosmology of *Yin-Yang chia,* complete with mystical calligraphic hexagrams, appeals to the aesthetic sensibilities. Taoist aesthetics is completed in Zen's yoga of *haiku* poetry and *sumiye* painting in which more than dream-like enjoyment is fostered: a way is opened for the devotee to intuitively grasp the values of life. An especially unique approach is seen in Zen's use of humor, an aesthetic category almost completely overlooked in most other religious models with the possible exception of certain ancient Hebrew tales.[3] Bergson's suggestion of a connection between laughter and moral insight may perhaps be applied to understanding Zen and Hebrew humor.[4]

Advaita Vedanta also stresses the aesthetic. Indeed, the entire phenomenal world is interpreted as a kind of "Brahma drama," a cosmic play, whereby all ethical problems are aesthetically resolved. It is possible that the aesthetic is even superior to the ethical. It does not seem, however, that finally the aesthetic is superior to the intellectual since the goal is really to understand (intellectual value) that life is a play (aesthetic value). Mahayana often seems to interpret compassion *(ahimsa)* aesthetically, and Taoism revels in the mystery of the aesthetic contemplation of the universe which finally culminates in a mystical vision in which the Sage "chariots on the Norms of the Universe and makes excursions into the Infinite!"

Existential Concerns

The problem of suffering and death is dealt with by the several naturalisms in a rather fatalistic and stoic manner. Jainism, Sankhya, and *Yin-Yang chia* view the universe as a kind of logical atomism which cycles with computer-like precision but apparently see no ultimate meaning in human anxiety about death. Tao Hsueh and Zen offer larger perspectives with their focus on *Ho*—harmony with the universe—including all our human concerns. But finally, even these systems relegate humanity's hopes, fears, and anxieties to merely incidental categories in the vast universe. The way out of anxiety is the path of discipline; some kind of yoga embracing moral, aesthetic, physical, and mental exercises. In the case of the Chinese and Japanese systems, aesthetic creativity seems to be offered as a solace for our anxieties about our finitude, but suffering and death have no answer that the human mind can comprehend. We can only cultivate inner strength and learn to accept the inevitable. No higher meaning is offered. *Satori*, in Zen and *nirvana*, in the negative sense of annihilation of the finite self, alone can bring peace.

For the monisms, suffering and death are, of course, not really real. He who suffers is under illusion, the spell of *maya* or the realm of *Yu* with its "shapes and features." The way to escape this illusion is, once again, self-salvation—to practice yogic disciplines and discover our true Self which is, and has always been, the Cosmic

Spirit (Brahman, Dharmakaya, or Tao). Experience union with this ultimate reality that neither suffers nor dies and all anxieties will cease. This reasoning is powerful and appeals to many individuals, but it has not eliminated the existential suffering from the human community in any phenomenal or historical sense. The most imaginative interpretation is found in Mahayana Buddhism where the altruistic and even sacrificial behavior of the Bodhisattva does seem to employ the law of vicarious suffering in the course of saving others from their suffering and anxiety about death.

The theisms see suffering and death as real, and the existential concerns of the individual are recognized as legitimate. What must I do to be saved? is recognized as a fundamental religious question. The individual is really threatened by loss of values, and the value most precious to each one—oneself—in biological death and possibly in hell! The loss of loved ones is a terrible possibility and one not able to be avoided. But suffering and death do not have the last word, as triumph over these evils is promised for those who enter into the right relationship with God and cultivate the proper spirit. The right relationship is one of faith and loyalty *(bhakti* and *hesed)*. In biblical theism this response comes in gratitude for God's continuing generosity to his less-than-deserving children. The proper spirit is love *(agape)* for all our fellow humans. This ethical love does not count the cost to self. In fact, evil may sometimes function as instrumental good for those who view the suffering through the eyes of faith. They may be challenged and strengthened in character.[5] Neither moral nor natural evil are God's intentional will. Rather they are his consequential will, given a universe fashioned in accordance with the logical laws. Most important, God's power and love are sufficient to turn even the darkest loss into victory for the spirit.[6]

Questions about human destiny and the meaning of history.

In the naturalisms, there is no transcendental vision pertaining to individual human destiny or human history in the large, and the goal is to escape from anxiety stemming from a misunderstanding of the true nature of the cosmos. Some kind of spiritual training or discipline is necessary. In Jainism and Sankhya, it is Yoga which enables one to gain control over life, body, and mind until the state of *moksha,* or release from ignorance *(avidya),* and the *samsara*

95

cycle are achieved. The *nirvana* is a kind of passionless peace in the negative, even nihilistic sense. The personality, the mind, no longer matters because the individual is only a temporary physical phenomenon without eternal value. The Tirthankaras possess all knowledge, but only in a computer-like, dispassionate sense beyond all caring are they omniscient. The beautiful *ahimsa* ethic finally is dropped off and has no further use or ultimate meaning. The Theravada system of Buddhism is very similar, and though there is a role for the *arhat* to play in terms of an interpersonal ethic, the religious goal seems to be largely egoistic. In Jainism and Sankhya the cycles of involution and evolution are repeated endlessly, with the process of sorting out *jiva* from *ajiva* or *purusa* from *prakrti* being the only purpose.

In Tao Hsueh and Zen, yoga takes the form of the aesthetic contemplation of nature and artistic pursuits. Calligraphy becomes a very precise aesthetic discipline and an aid toward understanding that *nirvana* is in every existential moment. There is no transcendent heaven or far-off historical goal. Nature's Tao spins out the wonderful cosmos eternally, and meaning exists only in the process itself. Though the universe is beautiful in the whole, ethical values must always remain relative, and no final judgment may be rendered about good and evil. The Confucian ethic perhaps stresses the good society in Tao Hsueh more than Zen, but even here, moderation and cosmic relativism are the regulative principles.

The monisms assert that Mind, or Spirit, lies at the heart of the universe as its Cause. It follows that persons have as their goal, individually and collectively, the attainment of Cosmic Spirithood, or unity with this Eternal Mind. Yogic discipline enables the *jivanmukta* to exclaim "Aham Brahm asmi" (I am Brahman!) and "Tat tuam asi" (You are It!). But finally, the experience of *satchitananda* (blissful cosmic consciousness of true being) is completely monistic because there is only One Self—Brahmatman. The value of finite personhood is transcended. It might also be observed that since time is unreal, history is illusory, and no genuinely new truths or novel creations emerge. In eternity, everything has already happened and is already known by the omniscient Self. There is an awesome sense in which the eternal now is absolutely static.

This seems to be the case in Mahayana also, only here Dharmakaya, or Buddha Mind, is the Ultimate One. The path to *nirvana* involves an ethical life of selfless service to all sentient beings rather than the detached intellectual contemplation of Advaita Vedanta. In later, mystical Taoism, the sage comes to forget distinctions and "sit in the center of the Tao" by way of mystic contemplation involving the aesthetic attitude. An historical social order has intrumental value only for the final state of cosmic consciousness and unity with Brahman, Dharmakaya, or Tao.

Only the theistic religions regard the finite person as having eternal worth. Judaism, Christianity, and the Vishistadvaita and Dvaita Vedantas of Ramanuja and Madhva (particularly as interpreted by Aurobindo and Radhakrishnan) proclaim that terrestrial, corporeal existence does not provide an adequate opportunity for the self-realization of persons and therefore posit an afterlife. The biblical models provide a transcendental realm (or realms) of heaven or hell as the theater for this continuing opportunity, while Vishistadvaita and Dvaita retain the traditional Hindu concept of cycling rebirths on planet Earth via *samsara*. Conservative biblical interpreters believe that a final judgment awaits each person at death, then final and permanent assignments to heaven or hell, but more liberal theologians suggest that judgment is a continuing crisis in our lives and that self-realization is an infinitely continuing process.

Both the biblical and the Indian models provide for the self-realization of persons in a developing community of ethical love. The Christian name is Kingdom of God; Radhakrishnan calls it *brahmaloka,* and Aurobindo details a community peopled by saints, each being "a poise of being for Brahman," where spiritual powers control matter so that all medical and energy problems are solved. Death is, of course, eliminated from the scheme of things. Christians testify to a vision of joyful, creative interpersonal experience which centers around intimate communion with the loving God-Person. There seems to be both a terrestrial denouement culminating in the divine society or, in Augustine's words, City of God, and a supernatural experience, i.e., heaven.

For the biblical theism, time is real and meaningful; history is holy—*Heilsgeschichte.* Humanity's existential concerns about personal worth, destiny, and the meaning of it all are answered with

97

the assertion that love and righteousness will triumph in history because the God who is lord of history is also the God who is love. The most impressive difference between this view and the other models is the emphasis placed on the finite person's freedom, spirituality, creativity, and limitless potential for self-realization. In this vision of eternity these values are not lost, sacrificed, or swallowed up in a Greater One. The love that grounds all and holds it all together is possible only in the context of the eternal I-Thou relationship. Perhaps this is why Buber makes this relationship his metaphysical ground.

Developing a Method of Evaluation in the Light of a Major Premise

The point in doing the philosophy of comparative religion, as we have said, is to gain a more comprehensive understanding of world religion through the use of critical philosophical analysis and speculation. Inevitably, value judgments will have to be made including the terms *true* and *false* and *good* and *bad,* properly qualified by the adjective *probably.* I make this point clearly because some recent attempts to do philosophy of religion emphasize analysis and clarification to the point of excluding any attempt to reach conclusions. Willem Zuurdeeg's statement still rings in my mind. "It is not the business of the philosopher to decide what is real"; "No proofs or arguments can be offered to show what is true. All we can do is witness to one another and invite others to live as we do."[7] It is the contention of the writer that though this point of view contains some truth about the impossibility of attaining absolute rational certainty and is an accurate description of religious behavior, it is not an acceptable approach to doing the philosophy of religion. If philosophy is not to become bankrupt, it must include attempts at verification as well as clarification and explication. We have carefully examined each of these categories in chapter 2.

The task before us now is to take a closer look at the data we have just correlated and evaluate it in terms of intrinsic worth and possible instrumental value for future development. In the course of our evaluating, we will employ presuppositions and standards that will inevitably reflect a point of view. We are reminded of Hare's concept of the blik and Kant's notion of the regulative use of a major premise like theism. There seems to be no escaping this heuristic leap, that is, the intuitive effort to see directly for oneself. We have already identified the perspective that guides the present analysis as personalistic in the discussion of personalistic syncretism in chapter 2.

In light of the plain fact that a person is at the center of all experiencing and philosophizing, it seems strange that it is even necessary to have to defend personalism, but the truth of the matter is that various kinds of naturalism, vitalism, phenomenology, and linguistic analysis seem to have temporarily eclipsed personalistic philosophy. Admittedly, humanism and various existential expressions contain much content found in personalism, but the metaphysical ground is either absent or not complete and often views about value, especially ethics, are distressingly vague or self-contradictory. While the purpose of this analysis is not to explicate the philosophical system known as personalistic idealism, it is appropriate and necessary to explain the major premise, or blik. A personalist is one who perceives, understands, evaluates, and commits himself on the major assumption that the category of personhood is the highest value because it affords the best understanding of the deepest intuitions, the most profound experiences, and the sharpest problems of humanity.

A shallow anthropomorphism is avoided by stressing the spiritual above the biological features of persons and leaving open the possibility of the existence of other-than-terrestrial persons. Principally, self-conscious awareness of identity; the capacity for rational, reflective thought, including memory, ethical discrimination, appreciation of beauty, and religious awe; and the capacity to love, purpose, and create are regarded as fundamental categories of personhood. As all these are also characteristics of mind and its ideas, personalism is usually regarded as a species of idealism or idea-ism. But we can employ the aforementioned categories in constructing criteria of evaluation without launching into an elaborate defense of idealistic metaphysics. Indeed, it would be better to avoid premature conclusions of that sort until we have given all the data fair hearing.

Now we must confess that our personalistic blik is neither finally verifiable in terms of absolute rational certainty, nor is it the only possible premise. It is just as possible to begin with the assumption that nature is the ultimate self-explanatory category or that impersonal energy in constant flux is basic or that each existential moment of experience is ultimate. These intuitions form the nucleus of religious language in the heuristic mode, and without a blik we could not begin to think philosophically. But we have already noted the place of verification in reflective thought, and we must recognize that even our bliks must run the gauntlet of our tests for truth. For as Hare himself reminds us: there are bliks and there are bliks, and not all are of equal value. We have to ask ourselves honestly to compare the explanatory powers of the several bliks. Again, no correct answers will appear at the back of the book. The answers will vary with the temperament and philosophical orientation of each person, but even allowing for honest differences, rational consistency and empirical coherence will do much to help sort out large ideas from trivial ones. In testing bliks, consider questions like the following. Which premise takes account of most of the data? Does this include the most significant data? Which premise allows us to answer the most questions? The most important questions? Which allows for the greatest harmonization of contrary data? Which comes closest to using the data without sculpturing facts to fit preconceived formularizations? Each reader owes it to himself or herself to check and recheck the personalist premise to be employed in this analysis as well as any and all other possible bliks. The writer has confessed his personal starting point and will now proceed to use it in developing the criteria for evaluating the data provided by the religions of the world.

The material content for this next step has already been identified in chapter 2, where we considered the several categories of philosophical analysis in terms of clarification, explication, and verification. Our first task was to correlate the data with the categories of explication; now we must determine on the basis of criteria of verification and our major premise orientation where the truest and most valuable insights lie. It is now appropriate to develop the idea suggested in chapter 2 regarding personalistic syncretism, which will function as a tool of existential verification. The categories of explication and verification will be ranked in order of their significance for truth testing the major insights of religious philosophy. The category of clarification is a matter of linguistic form rather than material content and applies across the board, so to speak, to every tradition equally and therefore need not be ranked in our hierarchy of judgment. Turning to the categories, let us see what appears to be of first order of importance for evaluating the data.

We should take seriously the arguments of Slater and Smith regarding the value of the phenomenological method and give attention to the subjective categories. I suggest that we first consider the nonrational category of mood. It is surprising and even frightening when we recognize the extent to which feelings almost beyond our ability to call forth, control, or dismiss, influence our thinking and acting. But existential philosophy has made this quite clear and has substantiated the claim with numerous examples in great detail. To be quite specific, I suggest that what William James has called meliorism, and what I shall call the melioristic mood, be the touchstone of our evaluation. My decision is based on the recognition of a kind of emotional continuum ranging from moods of soaring optimism and exhilaration to the depth of despair and depression about the state of and destiny of the universe and our place in it. Many have noted that the religious attitude often comes very close to being a practical attitude so dramatically expressed in various ways by the several religions as How can I save my self? or How can I escape meaninglessness, suffering, and annihilation? Accordingly, we will rank any datum highest which suggests an answer to this question and is compatible with the melioristic mood. Specifically, the melioristic mood will be present in any religious statement that suggests the desirability and possibility of trying to ameliorate the very real evil conditions that work to frustrate human self-realization.

This discussion of mood leads directly into the next category of existential concerns generally formulated as questions about the meaning of life and the destiny of persons here and hereafter. Our personalistic criterion will rank highest those orientations and codes of human behavior that seem to maximize opportunity for personal and group self-actualization and tend to subordinate perspectives that favor the subpersonal and inorganic realms of being. This existential concern about the nature and meaning of cosmic telos and human history will lead to questions about the mystery of human suffering and whether it is meaningful to speak about cosmic justice. Before these can be meaningfully addressed, however, one must assume an ethical attitude.

The ethical attitude, third on our scale, is called forth by existential concerns and supported by the melioristic mood. A personalistic focus requires an interpersonal morality grounded in ethical love. Duties to self spring from a healthy acceptance and respect for self balanced against honest self-criticism. Duties to others are a reasonable extension but also include that Kantian deontological dimension of "ought," which clearly sets off our personalistic ethical attitude from egoistic and even altruistic hedonism or utilitarianism. The kind of love here intended is characterized by respect, concern, and care for persons and is really best described as an attitude of intellect and will more than a mood or emotion. Hence, it is really *ethical* love. Any and all data that bear on the ethical attitude as we have defined it must rank high on our scale of values.

Other values follow close on our evaluative scale. Ethical values must be accorded first place for the reasons already offered. Notions like social justice and cosmic community would be meaningless without an undergirding ethic. But a balanced model of personhood requires aesthetic and religious value as well. Here the reader might understandably conclude that a philosophy of comparative religion must necessarily put the religious value first. Our defense can only be that there is a comprehensive and a narrow way of interpreting the term *religion.* In the broad sense, religion will include the moods, attitudes, and concerns already identified, so we really have put religion first. However, in the narrow sense, the term *religion,* or more accurately for our discussion, *religious,* refers to a specific, *sui generis* experience which Rudolph Otto has called "the holy," or "the *numinous.* " It is this more technical, restricted sense of the term that is intended here. It is admittedly difficult to be positive about ranking the "good" above the "holy," but we will offer the following reasons. First, much Chinese religious philosophy, rich in ethical content, knows little or nothing of an experience of the holy yet is richly personalistic. Again, Indian and biblical systems, though rich in the experience of the holy, also exhibit great sensitivity regarding the importance of developing an ethical life in an ethical community. Particularly in the prophetic writings of the Bible is it clear that the ethical and religious attitudes cannot be divorced. Very likely this conclusion owes much to the experience the Hebrews had with the amoral fertility cults of the Phoenicians. Weighing all this, we conclude that the idea of the "good" may properly be ranked above the idea of the "holy," not because one category is better or more worthy than another but because the one informs or gives content to the other.

With regard to aesthetic values or experiences of the beautiful, we note that in most accounts and analyses of religion, particularly the philosophy of religion, this very basic human capacity has been all but ignored. One exception, an earlier work, comes to mind. It is Elton Trueblood's attempt to develop an aesthetic argument for God in which he points out that the experience of beauty suggests an intuition of meaning expressed, which, in the case of natural beauty, is compatible with the idea of a cosmic intelligence or God. Professor William Dean has recently attempted to construct a theology of beauty based almost entirely on his contention that the experience of beauty alone is intrinsic, while experiences of the good are instrumental to the realization of a never-to-be-realized utopia and experiences of the holy are transcendental and utterly alien. A fuller discussion and reaction to this thesis will appear in a later chapter about values. The point remains that the present study will incorporate ethical, religious, and aesthetic values into the analysis. We shall endeavor to be especially careful to identify material that develops insights regarding the place of these three major values in the total pattern of religion.

Reversing the traditional approach, we put the category of metaphysical and cosmological questions last. We support this decision by once again referring to the practical, almost pragmatic nature that characterizes the great religions. This does not imply that great and ancient questions about ultimate reality and cosmic design are unimportant. One could justly assert that they are of primary importance. Indeed, our personalistic key is quite compatible with a particular metaphysics. We can justify our decision by making a distinction between much traditional philosophy, which focuses upon ontology and metaphysics, and the philosophy of religion, which has an anthropomorphic focus. The philosophy of comparative religion is an extension of traditional philosophy of religion and shares its human-centered concerns.

In assessing the worth of particular world views and metaphysical premises we will be guided by our personalistic perspective, which holds that persons and values are of supreme worth. We need not be dogmatically predisposed as to the specific nature of the world ground and its manner of generating and directing world process to hold to our contention that whatever its nature, the ultimate power must account for persons and be conducive to nurturing their self-actualization in the experience of values and especially the increasing realization of ethical love in interpersonal community.

Evaluating the Data

The Melioristic Mood

The cosmic naturalisms—including Jainism, Sankhya, Tao Hsueh, and Zen—and the spiritual monisms—including Vedanta, Mahayana Buddhism, and Taoism—measure up to our melioristic criterion only in a very limited sense at best. The objective cosmos is already at its normative peak so there can really be no concern about bettering it. The real problem lies in us, and it is our subjective condition that requires bettering. Certainly, the yogic, self-psychological analysis contributes a valuable feature to our model which centers on self-actualization, but these visions are truncated. They offer no promise of a cosmic-wide interpersonal community which must include ethical as well as mystical and aesthetic values. The mood that characterizes them is not really melioristic, that is, clear-eyed about evil while remaining hopeful about the future. In the case of Vedanta, its focus on the inevitable attainment of Brahman consciousness is surely the paradigm case of supreme optimism, but it is optimism in a special and strange sense as we will see in our analysis of ethical love.

The theisms all measure up to the melioristic criterion inasmuch as they recognize humanity's less-than-ideal condition but offer the hope of a future salvation that is conditional. Man must recognize his dependent condition as well as his unique potentiality and will to commit himself in an interpersonal effort that involves God and centers on solving problems that pertain to the self-actualization of persons. The fundamental personalism of these theisms accounts for their compatibility with hope for a better condition based upon human initiative and creative effort interacting with and grounded in divine love and saving power. We must identify whatever in theism accounts for this melioristic mood and give it priority over whatever in the naturalisms and idealisms frustrates it.

The Existential Questions

The concern about suffering and death is central in the monistic models, especially in Buddhism, but the solution offered in no way provides for self-actualization of finite persons. Victory over suffering and realization are for the Cosmic Self—either Brahmatman or Dharmakaya. If the ethical life has only instrumental worth, then this is acceptable, but if the ethical dimension has intrinsic value, then it follows that finite personhood must be an eternal feature of existence. Plainly, the individual person must not be translated into a Super Person. Even possession of cosmic perspective and the vision of all truth could not compensate for the loss of the ethical dimension of personal experience.

This conclusion is strengthened by a further analysis of the nature of the moral life. We must define it as having to do with justice at the least. Justice, in turn, requires that each person be concerned with the condition and needs of other persons. This concern is the very root of the phenomenon called love. With sound insight has the phrase *ethical love* been coined. To make the concluding point, none of the monisms can offer a rational model that retains the feature of ethical love because this can only be a phenomenon of an interpersonal community.

The theisms alone deal with the existential concern about suffering and death in a way that does not violate the eternal opportunity for the individual person to strive after creative growth and the enjoyment of values. Theisms posit an eternal community of finite persons, including the Divine Person, in which the key feature is ethical love. Death is not final; the person will have continuing opportunity for growth. Suffering is not final; the suffering caused by moral and natural evils will be diminished in the course of the moral and intellectual evolution of persons. Clearly, our model must incorporate this valuable answer to the principal existential concern.

Existential concern about the meaning of history is also best

105

answered by the theisms, which envision a cosmic evolution culminating in the *brahmaloka* of Vishistadvaita and Dvaita Vedanta or a "holy history" whose end is the kingdom of God on earth. The transcendental corollary is heaven (or hell, where the progress has been temporarily frustrated), defined as the ideal community of persons realizing ideal ends as discussed before. Neither the naturalisms nor the monisms offer such positive, satisfying answers.

Ethical Attitude

Paradoxically, some of the naturalisms do recognize the ethical attitude. Jainism and Tao Hsueh accord it a rather high priority as evidenced by the categories of *ahimsa* and *jen.* Zen and Taoism, however, do not appear to regard the ethical attitude with seriousness since insistence upon cosmic relativism precludes any normative ethical standards. In view of our acceptance of the ethical attitude as a major criterion, we must regard these two systems as being inherently deficient in this category, and whatever it is that grounds this weakness must be excluded from our normative model.

The monisms Advaita Vedanta and Mahayana Buddhism similarly make a place for ethical duties with respect to *karma,* the law of cosmic justice. Indeed, the concept of *ahimsa* in Buddhism goes beyond the personal and includes all creatures and nonanimal living organisms as well. This concept of reverence for all sentient creatures throughout the universe goes beyond Western theism and can serve as a powerful corrective force guarding against the tendency of personalistic models to become narrowly anthropocentric.

However, the ethical attitude generally finds its strongest expression in the theisms, where the very purpose of existence focuses upon an evolving community of social justice. Unlike the monisms, this ethical attitude has intrinsic worth and is not merely an instrumental value that gives place to the higher one of understanding cosmic spiritual truth. Though the monisms, especially Buddhism, will contribute much to our final model with regard to the ethical concern, it is to the theisms that we must look for the most complete expression of this notion.

Axiological Questions

Questions about value are next in order and we have already reached conclusions about ethical values. In the manner of aesthetic values the theisms are not very explicit. Indeed, they are clearly subordinated to the ethical and religious ones. The Second Commandment, prohibiting "graven images," and Kierkegaard's model of the three stages with the religious highest, the ethical second, and the aesthetic lowest, are classic examples. So influential has this mistake been that Western man continues to reap the sorrows associated with ugliness and the exploitation of natural beauty. This traditional neglect of the beautiful even contaminates his ethical efforts. It is becoming clear that violation of natural beauty courts moral evil. Here is at least the suggestion of an argument for the coalescence of values.

We have noted that the naturalisms, especially Tao Hsueh and Zen, and the monisms give prominence to the aesthetic dimension. There are both theoretical and practical values here. Certain cosmological problems find solution from the aesthetic perspective, and human self-actualization absolutely requires such nourishment. Our model will incorporate any feature necessary to ground this valuable insight about the aesthetic dimensions of being and existence. Conversely, it must exclude those features of Western theism that have prevented and frustrated its acceptance.

The Metaphysical Questions

The monisms and theisms provide for a metaphysical ground to explain the existence of the universe and its ultimate purpose. The Cosmic Mind of Mahayana and Vedanta and the Creator-God of biblical tradition give us reasons for nature's being at all and for its being what it is. The naturalisms, on the other hand, assume that phenomenal nature is its own *raison d'être*—a self-explaining phenomenon requiring no further explanation. Reason asks why, but naturalism replies only with answers about how. To some it seems almost a dogmatic position, frustrating and offending the inquiring mind.

The theisms offer an interesting argument based upon the premise that God is motivated by love. Indeed, Western biblical theism asserts that God *is* love. When this love is defined in terms of caring and sharing, the creation of the universe and a community of

107

persons capable of learning to function in and appreciate the world seems very reasonable. It is difficult to reconcile persons and values with a metaphysical ground that is less than personal and less than loving. This is where serious questions are raised with respect to the monisms. Brahman, Sunyata, and Tao are ultimately beyond all personal categories. This particular problem will be considered later. For the present, we note that our model will incorporate features suggested by the monisms and theisms with respect to metaphysical questions.

With regard to cosmological questions, biblical theism provides answers in terms of the miraculous and divine fiat. Much confusion and unproductive disputation in the Western tradition can be traced to misunderstandings about these concepts. Here, the naturalisms deserve high marks for their rational speculation about the ordering of the phenomenal universe, its processes and destiny. Much of their speculation is thoroughly compatible with the findings of science and deserves a place in the final model. The challenge would seem to be to find a way to harmonize the descriptions of the naturalisms with the explanations of the theisms.

Outline of a Provisional Normative Model

In this fourth and final step we will lift up the key insights from the reservoir of previously categorized and evaluated data and arrange them in a pattern or composition that will clarify the relationships they have with one another. The propositions and their corollaries will constitute a working, normative model for the philosophy of comparative religion. As we noted earlier, such a model could be used in truth testing and in developing speculation with regard to questions raised pertaining to comparative religion. A key point worth noting is that although presuppositions and speculation are admittedly a part of our model making, we have relied heavily on empirical data along every step of the way. Modern efforts at doing philosophy, even speculative philosophy, must try to avoid the scholastic error of relying exclusively on propositions derived from authorities and arranged by formal logic. We make no claim that our model represents static perfection. It is intended to be a provisional guide at best, constructed in the spirit Professor Bertocci calls "growing empirical coherence."

Propositions and Corollaries Regarding the Nature of Ultimate Reality and Relationship with Persons, Values, and Cosmos

Proposition Alpha, Symbol 道

The Ultimate Ground must be the source of all being and infinite potentiality. All phenomena, the nonpersonal as well as the personal, are grounded here. The strongest symbols supporting this insight are Tao, Brahman, and Sunyata. These concepts reject all attempts at specific definition, especially anthropomorphisms. Any Ground more narrowly or specifically defined would not serve as an explanation for the cosmos and our manifold experiences so rich in power and mystery. Brahmanism, Buddhism, and Taoism have generally grasped this basic insight and expressed it with greater force than the biblical religions.

Corollary 1: Mysterium Aestheticum, Symbol ॐ

It follows that a vast amount of phenomena emanating from or produced by this Ultimate must be classified as nonrational sense qualia and experiences rich in aesthetic and mystical qualities. We might label these awe-inspiring phenomena *mysterium aestheticum* and include categories ranging from the dreadful and demonic to the delightful and the ecstatic. This term is suggested because it seems to include more than just the experience of the Holy, which Rudolph Otto was identifying with his term *mysterium tremendum.* Taoism and Zen are especially rich in appreciation for the aesthetic, which ranges from the magnificent to the comic. The more somber and serious category of the experience of the holy can be illustrated with examples from each of the religions. The human response to the encounter with the awesome is succinctly symbolized by the familiar Sanskrit figure ॐ .

Corollary 2: Axiological Harmony, Symbol 氣

The aesthetic principle of organic unity seems to be operative throughout the cosmos and our experience of it. A kind of rhythmic harmony is presupposed by Tao Hsueh, which explicates the Tao in terms of the Yin-Yang dialectic. Chinese aesthetics refers to *Chi Yun,* or 氣 — "spirit of the Tao" or "rhythmic vitality"—the first canon for evaluating art.[8] *Ho,* the principle of harmony with all

109

A Normative Model of Ultimate Reality: Ultimate Ground and Its Relationship with Cosmos, Persons and Values:

EMERGING TELOS
Nature, Persons, and Values

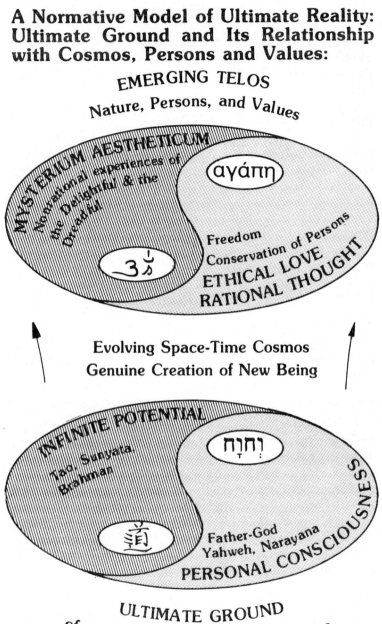

MYSTERIUM AESTHETICUM
Non-rational experiences of the Delightful & the Dreadful

αγάπη

3 ½

Freedom
Conservation of Persons
ETHICAL LOVE
RATIONAL THOUGHT

Evolving Space-Time Cosmos
Genuine Creation of New Being

INFINITE POTENTIAL
Tao, Sunyata, Brahman

וְרוּחַ

道

Father-God
Yahweh, Narayana
PERSONAL CONSCIOUSNESS

ULTIMATE GROUND
of all Being, Experience, and Values

things, is a prominent virtue of Tao Hsueh. This idea of a coalescence of all values in a universe that is finally comprehensively coherent is also a feature of the monisms, especially Advaita Vedanta.

Proposition Omega, Symbol וְחנָה

The final telos of the Ultimate Ground must include the maximization of persons and their values. This is necessary because self-conscious thinking, feeling, and willing persons are the highest values we know and are possible only if the Ultimate Ground possesses personal characteristics as part of infinite potentiality. The concept of the Ultimate must, then, encompass more than proposition alpha and include rational, personalistic symbols such as self-consciousness; identity that persists through change; capacity for rational, reflective thought; capacity to experience feeling and value; ability to purpose, will, and create. In sum, the Ultimate must, in addition to being Ground of being and infinite potential, be a Person, and the Ground of rational thought. This is the fundamental insight of the theisms, biblical and Indian, and it is most dramatically expressed in the theophany of Exod. 3:14 when God declares his name to be *Yahweh:* "I AM!" the Hebrew וְחנָה .

Corollary 1: Ethical Love, Symbol αγάπη

The chief manifestation of the Person God is *agape* love, which needs to be understood in terms of the moral law which, in turn, must be capable of rational explication. Closely associated with divine love is gracious forgiving and providential care. While this is central to the drama of Israel and Jesus' interpretation of the messiah, we have found close parallels in the concept of *ahimsa* and the compassionate spirit of the Bodhisattvas. In biblical, Indian, and Buddhist tradition love is always twined with ethical demands as the Decalogue, the Yogas, the Middle Path, and the Confucian Four Constant Virtues exemplify.

Corollary 2: Axiological Conservation

The conservation of values must be part of the final telos because it is reasonable to maximize quality and achieve as much actualization of potentiality as possible. Intellectual, moral,

111

aesthetic, and religious values will all be included in the hierarchy of values that must recognize persons as the highest value because no actual values can exist apart from personal appreciation. This means that there must be a law of the conservation of persons in a community of ethical love which alone gives sufficient reason for the existence of persons and human suffering and provides for the self-actualization of the Person God. The Vedanta of Madhva and the Christian hope offer the clearest and best examples of this insight.

With the construction of our provisional, normative model we have completed the task we set for ourselves in part I; that is, we have introduced a new approach to the study of religion and suggested parameters that empirical data and philosophical analysis suggest are to be regarded as, at least tentatively, true. In part II we set ourselves to the task of giving examples of actually doing the philosophy of comparative religion. The data suggest that there are at least three problems immediately identifiable as unique and basic to this new discipline.

Part II:
Special Problems for the Philosophy of Comparative Religion

We have reached the point in our project at which we can turn our attention to special problems that appear to be uniquely suited for analysis within the context of the philosophy of comparative religion. Probably, this discipline will prove to be open-ended with respect to the number and kinds of problems considered as more information and data are assimilated from the world religions. But we will make a beginning and identify what appear to be the most obvious and significant areas of interest for our study.

Both the theoretical and the practical aspects of philosophy and religion direct our attention to the areas of metaphysics and axiology. Accordingly, we are guided by our provisional model developed in the last chapter to formulate three questions. (1) What is the origin and significance of the triune patterns of the ultimate power found in the great religions of the world? We shall develop an answer in terms of axiology, specifically, human experience of the primary values. (2) What is the nature of ultimate reality? Specifically, what is the significance and relationship of the personal and nonpersonal data provided by the world religions? Here, we will work with a continuum of ideas ranging from the insights in Taoism to those found in biblical religion. (3) What is the nature and destiny of the person? Again, a spectrum of data regarding the ontological status of the person will be studied to see if it can be reconciled and provide us with a clue to a truer perception of what it means to be a person.

Chapter Five:
The Significance of the
Triune Patterns of Ultimate Reality

Our survey of religious data in chapter 3 makes it plain that all the great religions take a monistic or monotheistic form. The reason for this is that dualistic and pluralistic models raise more problems than they answer. From the perspective of reason, we find them unintelligible apart from a unifying world ground that integrates and harmonizes the disparate and dialectical forces. From the existential perspective we realize that multiple and conflicting feelings, loves, and loyalties can be harmonized only within the framework of a largest loyalty to the Ultimate One.

A closer look, however, reveals another common feature: the great religions develop and present their monistic or monotheistic premise in three-dimensional models called trinities. Traditional philosophy of religion pays scant attention to the trinitarian model of Christian thought, probably because it is regarded as an article of credulous faith not worthy of philosophical analysis, and traditional theology approaches the problem from the perspective of Christian doctrine, which ignored parallel models in the other religions. Comparative religion takes note of the phenomenon but is generally not interested in going beyond recognition and description. It would seem that the phenomenon of trinitarian models offers an exciting challenge for the philosophy of comparative religion. Indeed, we offer it as our first example of the special kinds of problems relevant to our new discipline. Let us phrase it this way: What is the origin and significance of the triune patterns of the ultimate power found in the great religions of the world?

Before we can construct a reasonable hypothesis we need to return to the religious data, this time to focus precisely on the trinitarian themes. The following summary will try to put before us what would appear to be the most significant data.

Trinitarian Themes in the Great Religions

Taoism

We have noted that the unifying concept is Tao, 道, the metaphysical ground and infinite potential from which all emerges and to which all returns. The mysterious Tao can be known only by a kind of mystical intuition and Lao Tzu's famous remark summarizes the matter tersely: "Whereof one cannot speak, one remains silent." However, the practical Chinese are not content to remain silent and seek to understand and explain the origin of the cosmos and its workings. This is why Yin and Yang, the female/male categories, are introduced into the Taoist model so beautifully diagrammed by the *T'ai Chi:* ☯. Some imagine two cosmic fish swirling round and round in the cosmic pool. Tao is the surrounding circle within which Yang and Yin produce the phenomenal, space-time world in a kind of sexual dialectic. All atoms and elements and things are their "children," and the recurring cycles of life—birth/death, good/evil, beauty/ugliness—are thereby explained. The Chinese Taoist trinity dramatizes a universe without beginning or end and is neatly summarized by the saying "One Yang, one Yin, that is Tao."[1]

Confucianism

We have seen that Confucianism, or *Ju chia,* is a philosophical ethic rather than a religious system of cosmology and soteriology—a practical, down-to-earth, no-nonsense kind of religion. It is a powerful, thoroughgoing humanism that finds its world ground in an encompassing naturalism. But it also must make distinctions in order to come to terms with the realities of the human experience.

116

We might visualize a kind of vertical dialectic with Earth—the naturalistic, biological forces of nature with which human beings must cope below—opposed by heaven or the moral laws and the sense of ought in the conscience above. Acting as a kind of synthesizing balancer is man, who when his potential for self-realization is properly nurtured is the *chun-tzu,* or "superior person," standing between the other two cosmic forces. Humanity can keep the cosmos in balance by practicing the Constant Virtues of *jen* (human-heartedness), *yi* (justice), *li* (propriety), and *chih* (wisdom). Skill must be developed to practice these in terms of *chung-yung,* the golden rule of doing ordinary things just right. The goal is *ho,* or harmony, which results when the trinity of man, heaven, and earth are in a state of perfect equilibrium. With respect to the earth, good ecology will be 天人地 practiced, respecting heaven; the moral law will be kept, respecting our fellowman; the golden rule of *chung-shu* (in the double sense of doing the good and refraining from doing the evil which we and others desire and abhor) will be honored.[2]

Brahmanism

We have noted that this religious/philosophical system is an expression of monistic idealism in which the intellectual concept of Brahman serves as metaphysical ground. Like Tao, Brahman is beyond all empirical factors and intellectual categories. But life as it appears on the phenomenal plane, though called illusion *(maya)* must somehow be explained. The generative, decaying, and persisting forces and features are accounted for in terms of the Hindu trinity, Trimurti. This trinity is composed of Brahman, the source of all (rather like Tao), which expresses itself in terms of Vishnu, the Lord of ethical and value-conserving power, and Shiva, the Lord of the cyclic process of birth and death. Often this is symbolized as a snake biting its tail—the *samsara* cycle. These lords or gods may be personified by *avatars,* or incarnations. The saviors Krishna an Rama are incarnations of Vishnu while Kali is the fearful, awful goddess-consort of Shiva.[3]

Buddhism

In Mahayana Buddhism the idea of Trikaya, the three Bodies of Buddha, was developed. Paralleling the concepts of Tao and

Brahman we have here the Dharmakaya, or the Body of Essence, which is the Buddha Nature beyond all possible conception or articulation. It is the Ultimate One which grounds all being—the Buddhist metaphysical first principle—within which function the Alaya-vijnana, pure consciousness.[4] There is an important difference from the first Person of the Indian Trimurti. Whereas Brahman is regarded as the neutral ground of all being, Dharmakaya is regarded as "a sort of love—behind—things that produces Buddhas—a Buddha essence at the heart of the universe."[5] The second mode of the Ultimate One is the Sambhogakaya, the Body of Bliss, which is the heavenly manifestation of the Buddha, conceptualized by thought as omnipotent, omniscient, and omnipresent. In the Buddhist heavens this Buddha takes the various forms of celestial Buddhas and Bodhisattvas. The third mode is the Nirmanakaya, Body of Manifestation (or Earthly Forms), which is the Buddha Essence as it appears during its earthly career. This earthly Buddha has as its intermediary the Sambhogakaya, from which it is projected. The greatest example is Gautama, whose life provided the impetus for developing the Buddhist trinity.

The Christian Faith

The Christian faith, like its parent, Judaism, is strictly monotheistic. But even though Yahweh is continually involved in history throughout the Old Testament stories, Christians believe that God's involvement in *all* dimensions of life needs fuller explication. The Christian trinity, nowhere mentioned in the scriptures, is a late theological model which attempts to deal with the problem. The phrase "God in three persons" is misleading today because our modern word "person" means an individual human being while the Latin word *persona* (the verb *persona,* literally "to speak through") and the Greek word *prosopon* referred to the masks worn by actors to define the various roles being played out. Hence, the phrase "God in three *prosopons* " was really intended to mean that God is playing three roles. The first role, that of "Father," does not mean tender fatherly affection but refers to the procreative power of the father. He is the ground of creation and in this respect may be likened to Brahman or Tao. The second role, "God the Son," refers to the divine love manifested in the man Jesus called Christ and focuses upon the moral and religious significance of the teachings and mighty works that characterize his life. The third role, "God the Holy Spirit," called attention to the mystical presence of God in the religious experience and especially to his function as "Comforter," or paraclete. Unlike human actors, God is regarded as playing all three roles simultaneously and eternally. Clearly, this doctrine does not assert the existence of three gods; nor is there a mystery whereby three is really one in this neomodalistic interpretation of the Trinity.[6]

Main Features of the Trinitarian Patterns

Every one of these trinitarian models identifies and incorporates concepts of great theoretical and/or pragmatic value, which include symbols of the ground of reality, creative power, evolutionary process, ethical source or moral law, the human-historical dimension, mystical-religious experience, and union with the divine.

The Taoist trinity focuses upon processes and manifold phenomena of nature, emphasizing the essential unity of humanity and nature. The great contribution here might well be awareness of the need to be sensitive about the need for ecological balance. But there seems to be lacking any specific ethic for humans. Nor are persons accorded any ultimate value with regard to the universe. The concept of Tao, however, as transcendent ground of all is a very powerful one.

The Confucianist trinity stresses human individual and social ethics with respect to nature and recognizes the experience of ought but suggests no significant transcendental reality or purpose. The positive characteristics of these two systems supplement their respective deficiencies in the classic system known as Tao Hsueh, or Neo-Confucianism, which offers a system of individual and social ethics within a naturalistic framework that stresses ecological responsibility.

The Indian trinity focuses on the ebb-and-flow quality of *samsara* and provides for the relating of divine powers to human existence by means of faith in the *avatars*. Moreover, mystical union with the One becomes a possibility with the practice of Yoga. But in the Advaita school, which is most representative of Vedanta,

119

we have noted that the community of individuals is swallowed up by the One Cosmic Super Person, and the dimension of ethical love must necessarily be lost in the absence of an interpersonal community with ontological status.

The Buddhist trinity emphasizes the continuity between the Buddha Essence, that is, the metaphysical ground of all, and its historical manifestations which touch the everyday lives of ordinary persons and even all creatures. The outstanding contribution here is the recognition that somehow love or compassion is intimately connected with the purpose of the existence of the universe. A weakness might be the failure to stress the genuine humanity of the earthly Buddha. Lacking this premise, it is difficult to defend the optimism of devotees who are inspired by their faith in the potential Buddha nature in every human.[7]

The Christian trinity recognizes the experience of metaphysical ground, divine activity in history, and mystical presence of God in the believer. Though strong in the area of history and its significance (unique in all the world religions, save for Judaism, its parent), it is weak respecting practical concern for and aesthetic appreciation of nature. Moreover, it does not seem as logically direct as Advaita Vedanta in solving the problem of relating a pluraliy of finite persons with the supreme, infinite Person. Its emphasis upon ethical love and the lofty status of the individual are perhaps its most positive features.

Toward a Solution

In attempting to reach a deeper understanding about the significance of these triune formulations, we must not be misled into settling for surface-level insights. It would not be difficult, for example, to suggest that a pattern of creating, sustaining, and rectifying or saving functions was the primary message of the models. Indeed, these ideas do seem to be intended in just about every case. But if we are willing to experiment and hold each trinity, like a transparency, up to the light of the total data constituting the mother religion from which that trinity is derived, we seem to find a new clue.

Each trinity seems to capture and symbolize the primary experiences of value found in the parent religion. At this point we can now put to use the provisional normative model of ultimate reality that we developed in chapter 4. Remember that the "evolving telos" was on the one hand defined in terms of the *mysterium aestheticum* which includes nonrational experiences of the beautiful and the numinous and, on the other hand, as the rational component that includes ethical love. The thought emerges, quite compatible with our working model, that the three primary values most closely associated with universal religion are the holy, the ethical, and the aesthetic.

We must once again review the religious data, this time in the light of our regulative axiological concepts to put this "clue" to the test. If it proves to be reasonable then we can press on to develop our conclusion. Our analysis will identify the primary values in terms of three modes: the numinous, the ethical, and the aesthetic.

God in the Numinous Mode: The Mystic's Ecstasy

None of the great world religions at their highest level of expression are without some reference to that peculiar experience of the beyond which we call holy. In every case, the authors seem to reinforce what William James has characterized as the ineffable or unspeakable quality of the experience. Even though the experience conveys insight or knowledge and is therefore noetic, to use James's terminology again, it is beyond our ability to speak about or describe the experience in very much detail. Our attempts at linguistic formulation will be noncognitive at most and pure gibberish at least.

In the Indian tradition, the Upanishads develop in some detail the mystical progression from waking, thinking states through contemplative sleep to the dreamless state of pure insight as symbolized by the letters in the dipthong AUM, written as the holy symbol ॐ. At the instant of religious climax, the devotee can only utter OM! and then remain speechless in the face of all analytic inquiry. He may later add, "Aham brahm asmi" (I am Brahman!) and "Tat tuam asi" (You are It!), but to all suggestions that Brahman might be characterized in terms of this or that quality, he will reply, "Neti, neti" (Not that, not that). The mystical experience of the One is ineffable.

Likewise in the Chinese tradition, Tao is the name that cannot be named. We are warned that the name that can be named is not the eternal name: The One must forever remain "beyond shapes and

121

features." Like Brahman, Tao is the ontological cause of the universe and all phenomena which only in theory can be grasped in terms of analytic thought. This power which brings all things into space-time existence does not itself exist; it is the great No-Thing about which nothing can be said in linguistic terms. Lao Tzu puts it most succinctly: "Whereof we cannot speak, we must remain silent." However, he adds, much to the relief of generations of philosophers and theologians, "Before we can remain silent, many words must be spoken."

Though each one of the great religions contain allusions to the religious experience, it is most clearly and dramatically part of personalistic theisms where this peculiar experience can be said to be the sine qua non for faith. Rudolph Otto is the philosopher-theologian who has given us the most extensive treatment of the experience, and his *Idea of the Holy* is a landmark in the phenomenology of religion. Students of his work are familiar with his categories of majestic power, creatureliness, living energy, demonic dread, and weird fascination, which constitute the absolutely unique experience of the holy. Beyond these symbolic expressions we cannot go, and the reader who is innocent of the experience of the *numen* is advised by Otto to read no further since the religious experience is indefinable, an ultimate category of experience, *sui generis,* and not reducible to any other terms.

The Hebrew scriptures contain excellent source material for this concept and, in particular, one thinks of Isaiah of Jerusalem who in the eighth century B.C.E. utters the classic expression of one gripped by the Supreme Power: "Holy, holy, holy is the LORD of hosts; The whole earth is full of his glory" (Isa. 6:3). Later on in this classic theophany, Isaiah cries out, "Woe is me! . . . for I am a man of unclean lips, . . . for my eyes have seen the King" (Isa. 6:5). Isaiah's experience of the holy is wholly autonomous and requires no support from either ethical or aesthetic sensitivities to give it substance and meaning. As Otto has noted, the worshiper is overwhelmed by the sense of being in the presence of a majestic power that is quite beyond his natural analytical ability. He feels compelled to worship and adores the mysterious power which he intuits to be the highest and most worthy of all aspects of being. It is not that he is coerced; rather his adoration is elicited by the magnificence of One beyond his understanding. In subsequent reflection, the worshiper will be able to rationalize this experience by referring to nature and the work believed performed by this holy power. He will explain that God is the highest order of being, that he created and sustains the universe, so, of course, God is worthy of adoration and service. It is all quite reasonable, but the actual experience itself involves no such rationalization.

Ezekiel's experience provides us with another good illustration of this phenomenon. When the theophany of Yahweh riding his storm cloud chariot bursts upon him, Ezekiel falls to the ground in holy terror. Only after he hears Yahweh say, "Son of man, stand upon your feet, and I will speak with you," does he return to a calmer frame of mind which enables him to interpret the divine encounter in intellectual terms. These examples from biblical literature illustrate our earlier point—that we are dealing with fundamental dimensions of value experience which are autonomously valid and include rational categories only for the purpose of explication after the fact. The experience of the holy is essentially nonrational, but this should not prevent us from attempts to use our rational faculty in order that we might come to comprehend the experience as well as we can.

God in the Ethical Mode: The Prophet's Oracle

Each of the great religious systems give significant attention, if not prominence, to the dimension of the ethical experience. We have noted that the classical form of Chinese religious philosophy, Tao Hsueh, incorporates the very significant ethical insights of Confucianism. As Fung Yu-Lan has noted, we may distinguish two focuses—justice and love—to be the guideposts. The emphasis upon the innate ability of any normal person to recognize the claim of the will of heaven, or *Ming,* suggests Kant's position regarding our natural ability to experience moral "ought" and Bishop Butler's classic sermons on our God-given endowment of conscience.

Meng Tzu certainly lays great stress on the "four beginnings," or natural human capacities, to recognize compassion, modesty, truthfulness, and justice which make it possible, through their faithful nurturing, to achieve the "four constant virtues" of love,

123

propriety, wisdom, and righteousness. Even Hsun Tzu, the pragmatic realist, while disagreeing with Meng Tzu regarding the original nature of man, recognizes and admits that man must and can struggle to reach this plane of ethical self-realization. For Confucianism, becoming a "superior man," *chun-tzu,* in terms of the ethical categories noted ought to be the supreme goal of every person.

Indian religious philosophy gives much emphasis to the concept of *dharma,* or ethical duties. The *ashrama* outline a fourfold pattern of stages along life's way that begins with admonitions to the young student to be diligent and honest, proceeds through laws regarding marriage and family life, canons of effective teaching in the middle years, and culminates with observations regarding the meditation of the aged wandering sage. The ethical content is most specifically identified in the ethical decalogue of *karma-yoga* which rather closely parallels the ethical portions of the biblical decalogue. First, the *yamas* identify the "thou shalt not's" of ancient Jainism: Do not lie *(satya);* do not be lustful *(brahmacharya);* do not harm sentient creatures *(ahimsa);* do not steal *(asteya);* do not be greedy *(aparigraha).* The *niyamas,* or positive "thou shalt's," include injunctions to cultivate the virtures of purity *(shaucha),* contentment *(santosa),* austerity *(tapas),* study *(svadhyaya),* and devotion to God *(Ishvarapranidhana).*[8]

The cultivation of the ethical life is a necessary component of Yoga which includes discipline of the body by means of strenuous physical exercises and rigorous mental exercises beginning with control of the mind *(dharana)* and progressing through meditation *(dhyana)* to deep concentration until the mind becomes absorbed into the Object *(samadhi).* Western practitioners of Yoga frequently overlook or are not interested in the ethical component and of course fail to realize in theory and in practice the goal in Indian religious philosophy.

We have seen that Mahayana Buddhism picks up the ancient concept of *ahimsa* (noninjury) from the Hindu tradition and develops it dramatically in terms of the Bodhisattva whose concern is to love and cherish not just persons but all sentient beings. Their task as helper-Buddhas on earth is to assist all creatures in the upward spiral toward perfection in the Cosmic Buddha, or

Dharmakaya. The unswerving practice of ethical love in all circumstances must characterize their behavior.

Noted earlier is the emphasis given the ethical dimension of life by the theistic religions. The concept of *bereth,* or covenant, structures the very heart of the Hebrew faith, which proclaims that Yahweh is an ethical deity who is always faithful to his word. From patriarchal times, the notion of integrity, or keeping one's word, has structured this ethically oriented religion. Abram enters into a *bereth* with Yahweh by means of a dramatic ceremony wherein he halves sacrificial animals and passes between them while holding a torch symbolizing that the Lord God is also entering the contract, which stipulates that the seed of Abraham shall inherit the Promised Land if they remain faithful to God.[9] Here is the germ of ethical religion which will forever set it apart from "pagan" religions and their capricious gods.

The ethical and religious terms of the contract are expanded and clarified in the several versions of the Decalogue beginning with the very primitive Covenant Code found in Exod. 34:11-28 continuing through the classical Decalogue in Exod. 20:1-17 and culminating in the ethical Decalogue in Deut. 5:1-22. The Mosaic tradition bequeathed to humankind a moral code of the highest order which admonishes all who would have fellowship with Yahweh to refrain from lying, stealing, coveting, adultery, and murder. We have noted how the great pre-exilic prophets of Israel developed their Mosaic heritage in terms of social justice and steadfast love.[10]

The Christian faith centers on Jesus the Christ who continues developing these ethical-religious themes by expanding the commandments to include the motives and desires that must be incipient to the overt act. In that section of the Sermon on the Mount called the higher righteousness we find, for example, "You have heard that it was said to the men of old, 'You shall not kill'; . . . But I say to you that every one who is angry with his brother shall be liable to judgment" (Matt. 5:21-22). The name *Jesus* is a varient of *Hosea* ("Yahweh saves") and must have been a reminder of the great prophet's vision of Yahweh as God of ethical but forgiving love. He must have frequently referred to that prophet of ethical love as is recorded in Matt. 9:13*a* and 12:7. Certainly his own name for God, "Father," strongly suggests

125

Hosea's beautiful poetic analogy of Yahweh as heavenly father in Hosea 11.

The union of love and morality finds continued expression with Paul who while proclaiming his freedom from Torah, enjoins believers to live lives characterized by ethical standards. His hymn to *agape* love in I Cor. 13 is a classical description of Christian love which is not proud, does not boast, and suffers all things for the sake of righteousness. This concept of *agape* as ethical love finds its highest expression in the Johannine literature. The author of the Fourth Gospel makes the Christ command his disciples to love one another even as God loves them. The fact that love based on affection like *eros* (desire) and *philia* (friendship) cannot be produced upon command points up that *agape* is regarded as having to do with an attitude under the control of the conscious mind and will rather than one subject to the whim of passing emotions. Erich Fromm has correctly analyzed ethical love in terms of intellectual understanding of the needs of persons, respect for them, concern for their self-realization, and existential commitment in their behalf.[11] In the First Letter of John we find the author proclaiming that God is to be understood in just these categories, for "God is love" (I John 4:8).

God in the Aesthetic Mode: The Artist's Vision

For some reason the aesthetic dimension has not been as fully developed in Western religious thought as in Eastern systems. It is, of course, true that there have been great and glorious artistic creations in painting, sculpture, architecture, and music which celebrate Jewish, Christian, and Moslem religious experience, but in general, Western religion tends to relegate the category of the aesthetic to a secondary status. Exceptions to this can be found in some of Israel's poetry ranging from the Song of Miriam, the Song of Deborah, and the erotic Songs of Solomon to the powerful oracles and moving hymns of the Second Temple. The great apocalyptic literature of Daniel and The Revelation to John also stand as monuments to the aesthetic expression of the religious experience. Nevertheless, even in these cases the aesthetic dimension is clearly subordinate to the ethical and religious experiences. Some have speculated that the Second Commandment, which so sternly forbids any attempt to create a visual likeness or portrayal of Yahweh, has functioned to frustrate a fuller aesthetic expression of Jewish, Christian, and Moslem faith until those religions moved outside the orbit of sole dependence upon literal obedience to scriptural command and were infused by the more permissive spirit of surrounding cultures in later eras.

Brahmanism combines abstruse philosophical speculation and intense psychological analysis with exciting aesthetic analogies. There is a sense in which Brahma is to be conceived as the Great Artist-Magician, who to escape eternal boredom, develops the play of the universe, in which he writes the script, creates the stage and scenery, and simultaneously acts out all the parts. It is all quite unreal; the word that describes this illusion is *maya,* from which we derive our words *mask* and *magic.* It is a marvelous magical costume festival full of colors, sensations, and sounds, and the endless flow of actors bear beneath their fanciful masks the common identity of the One. Intellectual and moral problems are not to be solved so much as they are dissolved in the blinding light of the mystical-aesthetic vision. Distinctions between good and evil, beauty and ugliness, even true and false, vanish in the light of the overpowering beauty of the *jivanmukta's* vision. Absent here is the telos of ethical love in the ultimate sense. True, ethical living and love are part of the good life, but finally such values seem to be instrumental only in leading the faithful to the only intrinsic value—the aesthetic vision—becoming conscious of the One. It is beauty that finally swallows up all intellectual paradoxes, moral dilemmas, and intolerable physical and emotional pains. *Satchit-ananda,* blissful cosmic consciousness of the truth, does indeed suggest the intellectual category, but the experience of truth is not to be analyzed and understood in the categories of Western epistemic dualism in which the thinker (subject) contemplates the object. The epistemic monism of Vedanta proclaims that subject and object become one and that knowledge is possible because of identity with, instead of contemplation of the object. Such an experience in Western terms is closer to ecstatic rapture, the *extasis theoria* of medieval Christian thought, than the intellectual experience.

The aesthetic experience seems to be most fully developed in Chinese Taoism and Ch'an Buddhism. Perhaps the unique Chinese system of written expressions has contributed much to this in that calligraphy consists of pictographs representing stylized snapshots of life which are best comprehended aesthetically. Fung Yu-Lan suggests that this intuitive ability, so necessary to the aesthetic experience, has been fostered in the agrarian people of China as a consequence of their close interaction with nature and its rhythmic processes. In any event, the emphasis is more often upon mental activity in terms of synthesis, required for recreating the aesthetic object in the mind, than analysis, required for metaphysical thought.[12]

When Indian Buddhism introduces metaphysical thinking to China and it is absorbed into Chinese Taoism, it finds a unique expression which draws upon aesthetic categories. The notion that Tao is the "Uncarved Block" elicits mental images of a great block of wood, stone, ivory, or jade being contemplated by a master artist-craftsman who imagines the infinite possibilities dormant within the block before he touches it with his cutting instrument. In another image, we might see the finished product emerging from the block by itself, unassisted by an artisan, and followed by a parade of creatures and objects without end. Even the aesthetic Indian analogy of the divine play does not match this for aesthetic directness, simplicity, and power.

Chuang Tzu is the master when it comes to calling forth aesthetic images. We have only to recall his dream of being a huge and beautiful yellow butterfly. So very vivid and convincing was the dream that Chuang Tzu was ever afterward haunted by doubts as to his true identity. Was he Chuang Tzu who had once dreamed of being the butterfly or was he really the butterfly now dreaming he is Chuang Tzu?[13] His playful aesthetic spirit is again demonstrated in the dialogue he had with his close friend Hui Tzu as they strolled across the bridge arching over the river Hao and contemplated the swirl of fish below. The master observed, "See how the minnows are darting about! Such is the pleasure that fish enjoy." "You are not a fish," said Hui Tzu. "How do you know what fish enjoy?" "You are not I," retorted Chuang Tzu, "so how do you know that I do not know what fish enjoy?" . . . "I know it just as we stand here over the Hao."[14] This delightful aesthetic playlet, of course, really probes into the problems of epistemic monism and dualism. In a final example, Chuang Tzu pictures the sage on a mystical flight riding on the chariot of the universe itself and making excursions into the infinite.[15]

As a whole, Taoism makes a powerful appeal to our aesthetic sensibilities with regard to nature. The order of nature is expressed more often in terms of beauty than by technical or metaphysical analysis. In support of this we need only recall the magnificent Taoist landscape paintings, which so successfully capture the spirit of mountains, woods, streams, and above all, space. Indeed, these scenes appear to be floating in and even emerging out of this space which is not empty and passive but vital and full of promise; like the Tao—ground of infinite potential.

Ch'an, later Zen, Buddhism picks up and develops this aesthetic theme in serious and comical expressions. The refreshing *haiku* poems and *sumiye* brush sketches represent Japanese stylization of the Chinese prototypes. Western people need to remind themselves that these religious philosophies of the Orient find expression in the arts so naturally that it seems strange and inappropriate to make a distinction between art and religion. Examples of Zen aesthetics may be found in Basho's matchless literary sketches which range from his famous phonetic description of the jumping and plopping old bullfrog to visions of the autumnal full moon reflected in the evening water.[16] We have earlier referred to sketches of Zen humor which play such an important part in explicating and eliciting and spirit of Zen. But in the case of humor as in all other aesthetic experiences, it is important to note that the point of a joke must be grasped intuitively, in a flash of insight. This view of the epistemological problem in which dualism melts into monism for an instant is fundamental to understanding the Oriental religious systems, and the closest analogy from their point of view is to be found in the aesthetic experience.

Resolution of the Problem: A Metatrinity of Values

Our in-depth review reinforces our intuition that the three primary values of the numinous, the ethical, and the beautiful can be interpreted as modes of experiencing the ultimate and indeed are found in each religious tradition. When we couple this fact with our earlier observation that each trinitarian model expresses the quintessence of the religion it symbolizes, we are led to see that the three basic values find expression in the models and this may be what accounts for their triune form. If this is the case, we can offer an answer to the original question. The triune patterns have their origin in the three fundamental modes of human experience, and the significance is that each trinity uniquely expresses human intuition of this phenomenon in such a way that dramatizes the dominant theme and incorporates the cultural style of the parent religion.

To confirm our thesis, let us hold the pattern of our metatrinity over each individual trinity and see just how the three basic modes are incorporated. The ethical mode will be seen to be represented by the following: Christos, Vishnu, Nirmanakaya, Chun-tzu, and Yang. The aesthetic mode by the Father-Creator, Shiva, Sambohgakaya, Earth, and Yin. The holy mode by the Holy Spirit, Brahman, Dharmakaya, T'ien, and Tao.

We are led to conclude that the various trinities can be best accounted for and understood by positing a kind of axiological metatrinity implicit in each religious tradition and metaphysical ground for all of them. It is important to recognize that this axiological trinity is best described in terms of a coalescence and not a hierarchy of values. At this point we must take issue with Professor William Dean, who believes that the correct path to reconstruction in theology is through the aesthetic experience. His analysis of experiences of the true, the good, the holy, and the beautiful lead him to acclaim the last as representing the highest order. Beauty alone is intrinsically valuable because it is

> realized in the subject's own present experience; it is not directed either toward what the objective case before the subject was [the true], toward what the future state beyond the subject will be [the good], or toward a reality that is wholly other than the subject [the holy].[17]

He denies that the experience of truth is intrinsically valuable and maintains that it is rather the instrumental usefulness of truth which we value. But this clearly is not consistent with our experiences of truth realization which carry a worth in and of themselves. We may indeed find use for a particular insight or bit of new knowledge and thereby confirm its instrumental value, but this in no way negates the intrinsic worth-in-itself of the experience. Similarly, Dean declares that our experiences of the good and the holy are instrumental only. "There is no moment for appreciation of instrinsic [ethical] value, but only a call for new instrumental action." Regarding experience of the holy he asks: "How can an experience (of the holy) that is conceptually vacuous function to provide the paramount orientation, the intrinsic value for an individual's life?"[18]

The record preserved in the data of the great religions suggests otherwise. There seems to be little doubt that the data purport to emphasize the fact that experiences of the ethical, holy, and aesthetic, all interpreted or reported in intellectual categories, are all to be regarded as having intrinsic worth. If this is true, then it will not suffice to develop a model along the lines of a hierarchy of values. That will lead to a false emphasis on some one value to the disparagement of the others. By positing a coalescence of values we avoid this error by recognizing that each value has equal worth.

Part of the problem may be due to confusion about the relation of instrumental to intrinsic values. It is not the case that if a value functions instrumentally it can never function intrinsically. We all know of instances when intrinsic values have also functioned instrumentally, as in the case of experiences of beauty and goodness being appreciated for their own sake while also serving to lead beyond themselves to an experience of the holy. Similarly, a religious experience of undoubted intrinsic value might work to lead one to experiences of goodness and beauty. We can express a rule here: all intrinsic values can serve as instrumental values, but, by limitation, only some instrumental values can function intrinsically. For example, money, as a medium of exchange, represents an instrumental value, but it cannot be correctly regarded as intrinsically valuable.

Our metatrinity of values suggested by the major religions does not elevate any one value experience above another but allows each to stand forth as autonomously valid. However, it is in their several combinations and supremely in their coalescence that the highest order of human experience emerges. Each religion gives a place for each value, though not in any sense are they given equal emphasis. It would appear that each system tends to emphasize one kind of experience above the others as it formulates its trinity in order to give symbolical expression to its unique intuition of ultimate reality. We turn now to our second problem, which is, How are personal and nonpersonal elements related in ultimate reality?

TRINITARIAN MODELS REFLECT THE PRIMARY VALUES

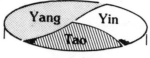

T'ai Chi

Trikaya

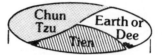

Tao Hsueh

Trimurti

Trinity

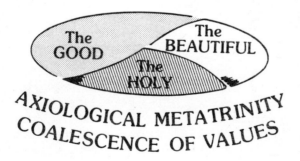

AXIOLOGICAL METATRINITY COALESCENCE OF VALUES

Chapter Six:
Personal and Nonpersonal
Dimensions of Ultimate Reality

Traditional philosophy of religion devotes a good deal of effort and space to discussing the ancient question as to whether or not God exists. Over the centuries we have come to recognize three arguments as classic: the ontological, the cosmological, and the teleological. Counter arguments offered by atheists and agnostics usually build upon the so-called problem of evil, while naturalists will argue that nature is a self-sufficient, self-explanatory category needing no transcendent deity to call it into existence. More recently, the analytic philosophers have charged that all contestants are guilty of misusing the language and have suggested a variety of more desirable ways of interpreting and using religious language.

The religious data we have compiled lead us to suggest that the philosophy of comparative religion follows a quite different approach to a consideration of ultimate reality. Recall that none of the data addresses itself to the question of the existence of the Ultimate since its reality is tacitly assumed in every tradition. The reason for this is twofold. First, there is the assurance based upon what is believed to be intuitive experience, revelation, or enlightenment, and second, any intellectual speculation must begin by positing the existence of an ultimate category as the major premise for further argumentation. It is just as clear from the data that the several religious philosophies offer models of ultimate reality that differ from one another quite radically. So, if we are perhaps misusing our time and energy when we argue over the traditional question about God's existence, it is quite clear that we are getting directly to the point when we ask, What is the nature of ultimate reality?

In preparing to answer this question, we turn again to the tentative model of ultimate reality that was suggested by the empirical data. We can gather up all the basic insights from the several religions and arrange them as a continuum of ideas ranging from the nonpersonal depths of pure potentiality and extending all the way to ideas of a personal God. Using this schema as a base line, we will arrange the several concepts in order and scan them for the purpose of identifying philosophical strengths and weaknesses which, taken together, might lead us to a more complete and truer understanding of the nature of ultimate reality.

Ultimate Reality: Pure Potentiality Without Distinction

Chinese Taoism provides us with the best model of ultimate reality conceived as pure potentiality without distinction. The first advantage of this concept is that it bypasses the trap of restrictive definitions; the second advantage is that by conceiving of Tao and No-thing, "beyond shapes and features," it avoids having to prove the Tao exists in space-time. But let us take a closer look at the problem posed by the refusal to offer a definition of Tao. Beyond the metaphorical phrase "Tao is the Uncarved Block," we are discouraged from asking for even a very permissive, provisional definition of Tao. We are reminded that only what is finite is subject to definition, and because Tao is infinite, it is beyond definition. We must be content to understand it as infinite potentiality and refrain from imposing restrictive definitions. "The name that can be named is not the enduring and unchanging Name" (*Tao Teh King* 1:1).[1]

Now granting that no definitions beyond logical and mathematical games can ever be complete, and admitting that, certainly, the ultimate principle of the universe must escape finite human formulations, we must nevertheless point out that in the absence of even a minimal definition, it is going to be very difficult to engage in cognitive speculation and analysis about problems relating to the Tao. We are driven necessarily back to what the sages claim are mystical intuitions of reality. Without faulting intuitive perceptions, we can assert that in the absence of rigorous testing by rational inquiry, we can never get beyond psychological certainty and into the realm of probable reasonable certainty. Of course, a great mystic like Chuang Tzu would be the first to admit this, probably with a smile as he sipped his tea.

The situation may not be beyond saving, however, because we recall that there were earlier periods of Taoism in which Tao was first equated with nature and later as the orderly and predictable processes which cause nature to behave as it does. Principally, we remember Lao Tzu's vision of the rhythmic, cyclic process that can be discerned throughout the natural order of things. Birth and death, growth and decay, thus have their place in our comprehension of Tao. So even though the original premise remains grounded in intuition, we are able to support it with observations drawn from the empirical world, formulated by rational thinking. Nevertheless, the concept of Tao remains the most obscure example of a model of ultimate reality in our collection of data from the great world religions.

When we press our study of this model with respect to its explanatory power regarding the existence of the universe we become aware of the strangeness of the concept. Assuming a principle of adequate causation to account for the world and finite persons, we look for an ultimate metaphysical ground that can be their cause. In the absence of a cosmic demiurge or artisan and a clearly defined telos, we cannot associate Tao with either efficient or final cause. The closest we can come to employing traditional Western categories of causation would seem to be to identify Tao with material and formal causes because it is the source of the world-stuff and the principles ("tao" with a lowercase "t"), which structures the organization of things. We can allow, then, that Tao does provide us with at least a limited explanation for the universe in terms of Western categories of analysis.

But in the context of Chinese thought, the concept of Tao makes no attempt to explain the existence of the world and the destiny of finite persons. It may be that we can accept the idea that Tao, as

136

infinite potential, accounts for the universe in all its magnificent diversity, but this is not to gain an understanding of why nature is the way it is, or, indeed, why it is at all. It would seem that the closest Taoism can come to answering Heidegger's famous question, Why is there something rather than nothing? is to suggest: Because it is possible! At best this suggests a kind of necessary emanationism with Tao unfolding mechanically until all possibilities are realized, followed by repeat performances ad infinitum.

But perhaps we have not been completely fair to this great tradition inasmuch as we have omitted the aesthetic dimension which, we have previously noted, occupies an exalted place in Chinese thought. The notion of mechanical emanation scarcely does justice to the artistic venture. Perhaps it would be better to speak of the unfolding of aesthetic possibilities. But as to why nature is so thoroughly characterized by aesthetic order, no reason is offered. It is simply the characteristic way of expression for Tao. Theists might conjecture that just as love is the essential attribute of the traditional Western model of God, so beauty must be the fundamental nature of Tao. But as we have seen, to attribute even this noble value to the ultimate is not allowed.

With respect to the human scene, Tao offers no comprehensive standard of ethical values that might guide us in our personal and social relationships beyond admonishing us to follow the natural way. We found *wu-wei* to be the golden rule and interpreted it to mean to live without stress as we engage in doing only that which is necessary for modest living, thereby avoiding unnatural overdoing. Such "doing by nondoing" and "creative quietude" will promote the good life, which is defined as being in harmony with the rest of the cosmos.[2] When we include the traditional Chinese appreciation for and skill in creating the beautiful, we can appreciate the great value for living that is inherent in this perspective. However, reverence for beauty and a graceful, poised style of living is not to be equated with the kind of ethical concerns so specifically identified in the biblical and yogic traditions. Reverence for the truth, justice, and care for other persons are certainly not absent from Chinese religious philosophy. Indeed, it may be argued that social concerns are central, but they have their origin not in *Tao-te chia* but in the *Ju chia* of Masters K'ung and Meng. Clearly, the model of Tao does not provide us with a foundation on which to build an ethical code. The fact that the great Chinese synthesis of Tao Hsueh incorporates the noble ethics of Confucianism only testifies to the consummate ability of the Chinese to work out a practical synthesis.

An overview of the Taoist model of ultimate reality reveals two very strong features: First, as we have noted, the phenomenon of the beauty of nature is singled out for special attention. Pragmatically, this emphasis has served to nurture the creative spirit in the Chinese people who have given aesthetic expression to that which ranges from the minute and insignificant to the majestic and tremendous. The aesthetic accomplishments of their culture have influenced all of Asia for two millennia and more recently are finding appreciation in the West. One looks for parallel accomplishments stemming from other models of the ultimate and, of course, finds that aesthetic expression is universal. But concepts of Brahman and Yahweh have just as often served to frustrate the aesthetic spirit. The extreme asceticism associated with certain yogic practices and the overly rigorous interpretation of the second commandment, "Thou shall not make for yourself a graven image," have often served to stifle aesthetic concern and expression. Monarchical models of deities have inspired some zealous followers to misinterpret moral codes in the spirit of vindictiveness quite incompatible with the disinterested attitude so necessary for the aesthetic experience. In our earlier discussion we admitted to the value of the pragmatic test while recognizing its limitations. Certainly, the Taoist model of ultimate reality deserves thoughtful attention in view of its favorable influence upon the human spirit.

The other commendable feature of this concept of reality has been its power to stimulate some persons to an acute awareness of the intimate relationship that obtains between humanity and nature. If man's importance is so underplayed that even his ethical duties are merely implicit in the teachings of Taoism, the other side of the coin is to lay the heaviest burden of responsibility upon us to make respect—even reverence—for nature our highest duty. Any abuse of things—animate of inanimate—in the natural order is an offense to the Tao which will entail untold consequences for us. Ages before the word *ecology* was coined, Taoism warned about getting out of step with nature's way and taught that peace and prosperity are intimately related to our developing a harmonious relationship with nature. One wonders if the radically contrasting biblical assertion attributed to Yahweh that we "multiply and subdue the earth" has played a part in the West's rather sorry history with regard to our abuse of nature and the resulting ecological and demographic crises that may very well pose as real a threat to our continued existence as the nuclear sword of Damocles that hangs over us does.

Ultimate Reality as Impersonal Power

The next point on our continuum of models of ultimate reality carries us beyond distinctionless potentiality and introduces some positive concepts which are best articulated in several Indian systems.

We learned in our earlier analysis of the data that ancient Dravidian thought sought to understand the cosmos in terms of a power struggle between spirit *(jiva)* and matter *(ajiva)* dramatically formulated in the religion we have come to call Jainism. Both these primeval forces represent impersonal power; even the life force is more like energy than what we might call conscious spirit. Following Zimmer's suggestion, we interpret the orthodox Indian system of Sankhya as a later Aryan development of the earlier Dravidian insight.[3] Now we have the primeval matter called *prakrti* and the primeval spirit called *purusha.* In this interpretation, their dialectical intercourse is productive of our universe rather than a battlefield where spirit struggles to shake off the tyranny of matter. Unlike Taoism, Sankhya gives us positive concepts explaining how *prakrti* and *purusha* cause the space-time universe to emerge. We saw earlier that we can define *purusha* in terms of formal and final cause and *prakrti* as material and efficient cause. As we noted, there is a reverse evolution in which all that is potential in *purusha* calls forth the actual material phenomena from *prakrti.*[4] But this grand process seems not to involve any conscious purposing mind—indeed, mind, or *mahat,* is just another emergent—and the eternal cycles of evolution/devolution suggest a mindless fate more than the journeying of an adventuring mind.

We have noticed a parallel in the Chinese system of *Yin-Yang chia,* which also conceives of the universe in terms of a dialectic between two primeval forces—in this case, an eternal male and

139

female encounter that produces the children-elements of our world. Once again, though this example of cosmic naturalism is more explicit about the generation of nature than the mode of Tao, it, like Sankhya, leaves us with a completely impersonal concept of ultimate reality. We should note that personal-sounding terms *Yin* and *Yang* are not to be taken literally but are intended to be symbolic of the active and passive qualities believed to make up our universe.

Both these systems—Sankhya and Yin-Yang—go beyond the Taoist model of ultimate reality in offering quite detailed descriptions as to how the universe gets to be the way it is. The advantage these models enjoy over the Taoist one derives from their introduction of positive concepts such as describing *prakrti* in terms of the three *gunas,* or qualities of matter, *tamas,* inertia; *rajas,* activity; and *sattva,* tension or harmony. Similarly, *purusha* is conceived as the ground of potential, but unlike the Tao model, the manner of its acting upon the *prakrti* to elicit gross and subtle substances and the phenomena of suprapersonal experience *(Buddhi* or *Mahat),* egoity *(ahamkara),* thought *(manas),* and the motor organs of persons is precisely identified. There is nothing vague about the Sankhya model, and if one studies the complex interacting patterns of the trigrams and hexagrams, the Yin-Yang model seems equally precise. But neither offers an explanation as to why there is a universe at all; nor do they suggest a *purpose* for existence beyond a rather meaningless eternity of expanding and collapsing universes.

It would seem that the only way to include purpose in the discussion and thereby offer a genuine explanation as opposed to description, is to frankly admit that there is a personal element in ultimate reality. This appears to be a self-evident point when we reflect that the notion of purpose is just about as basic to the human experience as is self-conscious awareness. One could hardly claim that a computer can purpose; rather we would be correct to say that calculating machines reach the conclusions necessary in view of their programming, and that puts the purposing back where it rightfully belongs—in the mind of the person who designed and programmed the computer.

Both Advaita Vedanta and Mahayana Buddhism offer models of ultimate reality that include this personal category of purpose. In

Vedanta, the concept of Cosmic Self, or Atman, becomes an important part of the ancient Brahman concept, and the result is Brahmatman, which may be, as Zimmer suggests, the most important accomplishment of the ancient Aryan *rishis,* or seers.[5] Similarly, as Buddhism became increasingly involved in a dialogue with orthodox Indian philosophy, the Mahayana school split from the older Theravada system and its naturalistic metaphysics and, following Vedanta, introduced the notion of Dharmakaya, the Buddha Mind, which we have noted is the first mode of Trikaya, the Buddhist trinity. Now, we have seen all this earlier, but the point of the review is to pinpoint the details as to how the notion of mind gets incorporated into the model of the ultimate. The reason for doing it includes the need to explain the existence of the universe in terms of purpose. The Advaita and Mahayana models can now assert that the universe exists because it fulfills the purpose of the Absolute to actualize its infinite potentiality. The dimension of mind that is now part of the model permits the use of the word *purpose* in a way that the model of Tao cannot. Moreover, the new model also goes beyond the Sankhya and Yin-Yang models because, as we have seen, their mechanistic quality really is not compatible with purpose. The modified model allows for the idea of a cosmic mind, purposing an evolving universe inhabited by finite persons who strive to understand their true identity and role in the cosmos.

But in achieving this fuller vision of the universe, has not a boundary been crossed so that we are no longer on the subject of this section, namely, ultimate reality as impersonal power? Haven't we moved along our continuum a point or two? The answer is no—not at all—because both Advaita and Mahayana make it clear that, so far, they have only been making concessions to imperfect human thought. We have been directing our attention to the Apara, or "lower" Brahma, which is transcended by the Para, or "higher" Brahman.[6] Similarly, Dharmakaya is more precisely interpreted as Alaya-vijnana or even Sunyata—the Void.[7] We must not attempt to apply any definitions—certainly not anthropomorphic ones like "personal mind"—to Brahman or Alaya-vijnana. The term *pure consciousness* is employed with respect to the Buddhist ultimate, and *satchitananda*—blissful cosmic consciousness of true being—is association with Vedanta's vision of the Absolute, but *consciousness,* in this sense, seems to be suprapersonal. In view of the fact that many of us have no experiential data that would help us clarify and verify this concept, we seem to be driven to the position of associating the "higher," "pure," and "supra" mind-like-but-not-mind phenomenon with our earlier view of the sophisticated cosmic computer. And, of course, this brings us back to our original theme that ultimate reality is impersonal power. But if our earlier observation about the concept of purpose requiring the larger frame of personal mind is correct, then there is a fatal flaw in these models of the Absolute. We cannot have it both ways: we cannot have purpose—so necessary if we are to have an explanation for the cosmos—and at the same time hold that the ground of that purpose is impersonal force.

However, we can identify some very strong features of this second group of models. First, Sankhya, Yin-Yang, Advaita, and Mahayana all work with a model of ultimate reality that enables those systems to give adequate recognition to the universe in its manifold expression, and they offer ingenious descriptions of how it behaves. With respect to cosmogenesis, mystery is played down, quite unlike Taoism, and evolutionary theses are boldly proclaimed. This is worth noting when we reflect how the doctrine of *creatio ex nihilo* of traditional theism has been interpreted until relatively recently as excluding the idea of evolution in any form whatever. The terrible conflict between science and religion which has plagued Western culture for at least three centuries has no parallel in Eastern experience because from earliest times, the idea of an evolving universe has been considered reasonable.

The Taittiriya Upanishad, of the eighth century B.C.E., gives us one of the earliest written expressions of this. Later, followers of Sankhya and Vaisheshika disputed about the details of the evolutionary process. The former have developed the doctrine of *satkaryavada*—the pre-existent effect—which might be likened to Western materialism's view that each succeeding stage in evolution is merely a necessary resultant and, conversely, reductionism applies to nature at every level so that, finally, any phenomenon is nothing but matter in motion. The latter group argues for *asatkaryavada*—the *not* pre-existent effect—which more closely parallels Western naturalism with its recognition that in addition to resultants, there are also emergents, which as

142

unpredictable phenomena, represent cases of genuine novelty in the course of evolution. They would also reject reductionism in the sense that every stage of the process provides us with examples of real phenomena incapable of being defined in lesser or lower terms.[8]

The hypothesis of an evolving universe is a very valuable one because it avoids a credulous, magical worldview which as we noted earlier, is bound to clash head on with the attempt to understand our experience of the cosmos in a reasonable way that, today, is consistent with the attempt to construct a scientific world view. Modern people can no more turn their back on their scientific heritage than they can renounce their religious legacy. Either way will lead us down and away from our telos of self-understanding and responsible living.

Ultimate Reality as Conscious Spirit

At this next point on our continuum of possibilities, we move to a consideration of a model that unequivocally conceives ultimate reality as a conscious spirit. The Vishistadvaita Vedanta of Ramanuja asserts that nature and persons are in no respect *maya* but are in fact realities that manifest the cosmic consciousness of Brahma. We have got beyond the idea of a "higher" Brahman that is somehow beyond the empirical realm of nature and categories of conscious thought. This interpretation of Atman, or Cosmic Spirit, is perfectly compatible with the positive attributes of intelligence and other characteristics of mind and so escapes the dilemma we discovered in Advaita with respect to purpose. This modified Vedanta can affirm without contradiction that Brahma purposes the world of nature and finite persons. The universe does not emerge mysteriously out of infinite potential; nor are unconscious mechanical forces accorded that honor. The ultimate is not first explained as possessing consciousness in some metaphysical sense, then, later, said to be really something beyond consciousness. In this view the ultimate is really, and unequivocally, a conscious spirit.[9]

Let us briefly recapitulate the salient features that we earlier compiled. Vishistadvaita Vedanta, or qualified monism, develops a model of the ultimate in three modes: Brahma as (1) the eternal ground of all being; (2) the eternal realm of nature; and (3) the

143

eternal community of persons. Each mode is as equally real, eternal, and identical with Brahma as the others. All three modes together comprise the model of the Absolute.[10] Ramanuja has the best of both worlds: he has retained the powerful monistic major premise of Advaita Vedanta and also the valuable view that the world and finite persons, responsible for their ethical choices, are real. This last point is especially important because it allows for the ethical dimension of experience to have eternal, intrinsic value. In previous models, either the aesthetic or intellectual value was accorded first place while the moral life seemed to be relegated to the status of instrumental value.

In fact, the chief advantage of this model over the others seems to be that now we have the notion of the telos or grand purpose for the existence of the world, which is that there shall develop an ideal society of persons living in perfect harmony with one another and with nature. The modern Indian philosophers Radhakrishnan and Aurobindo, incorporating ideas from Vishistadvaita, present us with a scenerio of this developing ethical society that is consistent with human choice. This realm or community of saints Radhakrishnan calls the *brahmaloka,* or kingdom of Brahma. Aurobindo refers to the members of the kingdom as "gnostic beings"—superior creatures soon to emerge with the next stage of evolution. Each one of these saints will know himself to be a "poise of being for Brahma" exemplifying the highest virtues and enjoying *satchitananda.* Thus, this model grounds a vision of persons in community which is noble and optimistic.[11] This eschatological vision may be regarded as a genuine telos as it avoids the traditional view of Vedanta, which holds that after such perfection has been reached, devolution, or a kind of going back to square one, follows with the whole evolutionary process being repeated ad infinitum. At least the modern interpretations of Radhakrishnan and Aurobindo envision a continuous realization and enjoyment of the powers of the Absolute in the phenomenal world.

But for all its strength, this particular model of ultimate reality as conscious self nevertheless leaves us with a major philosophical problem—really the classical question about the one and the many. We grant that the introduction of qualities of spirit of selfhood eases the original problem about seeing the existence of the universe in terms of purpose, but now we have to try to understand how the One Absolute can, at the same time, also be three eternal modes—each one just as eternally real as the others. The logical laws, of course, require that anything must be what it is and not something else. The model of Brahma as conscious self, finite persons, and impersonal nature—simultaneously—seems to fly in the face of these time-honored rational principles.

A reasonable way out of the difficulty would be to understand the logical laws to mean that anything must be what it is and not something else *in the same respect and from the same perspective.* This will allow us the logical possibility of conceiving of the Unified Self from other perspectives in which it manifests itself as human community and natural order. There would no longer seem to be any logical difficulty about regarding the material universe as an eternal expression of the Cosmic Self. But what about the logical integrity of the concept of this same Unified Self simultaneously having the multiple experiences of the community of finite selves? We might turn to an analogy drawn from our everyday life situation in which each of us plays several different roles, e.g., son or daughter, brother or sister, parent, teacher, etc.—all the while remaining the one same person. Perhaps in this way we can comprehend how the community of finite persons are really expressions of the One Self. But this analogy directs our attention to three other problems.

1) We do not regard the several roles we play as being independently real and self-sustaining. These roles simply could not exist apart from the center we know existentially to be our personal self. It is this center that is fundamental and primary to the other expressions of our personality and places in society. The roles are derived from and secondary to the existential center. But, returning to our original analogy, this suggests that the Cosmic Self is primary and most real while the finite selves are dependent and have only a derived reality. This would effectively deny the contention that the community of finite persons is an eternally real mode of ultimate reality.

2) It is the nature of human experience that at the center of our personal consciousness we know all about the various roles we are playing, and conversely, we are not ignorant about our true self at the center from the perspectives of these various roles we play. But once again our analogy seems to break down—at least with regard

to the converse clause—because irrespective of whether the Ultimate Self knows finite selves or not, it is quite clearly the case that most of us do not experience ourselves as the Cosmic Self of the universe. Even if we allow, as the Vedantins maintain, that *avidya,* or ignorance, blinds us to our true identity, the force of the analogy is much weakened.

3) Most serious of all, if finite persons are really identical with the One Self, then what we experience as our independent and finite freedom is illusory and the moral and intellectual dimensions of life become impossible. We would need to ascribe to the One all the confusion, ignorance, and evil which often characterize our mental states. In short, the Cosmic Self would be involved in a conflict of mental concepts which, paradoxically, it is eternally thinking. We have come full circle and are once again back to stretching the logical laws beyond endurance. A unified mind simply cannot think X and non-X simultaneously. Within the parameters of the model of ultimate being as Conscious Self as developed by Vishistadvaita we seem to have encountered unsurmountable problems when attempting to identify the experience of finite selves with a universal Self.

Ultimate Reality as Cosmic Person

We come now to a consideration of theism which marks the terminus of our continuum of possibilities. It will be helpful at this time to refer to the thought of Dr. Peter A. Bertocci, a contemporary spokesman for philosophical personalism. He articulates the major premise very clearly: "The personalist holds that the self-sufficient cosmic Unity-Continuity is, like the finite person, a Knower, a Mind or Spirit."[12] Just as clearly, Bertocci honestly recognizes and recites the criticisms that have been leveled at personalism, beginning with Xenophanes' wry observations that Ethiopians conceive of a black deity and Thracians depict one with blue eyes, continuing through Spinoza's exercises in deanthropomorphizing to Tillich's rejection of a personal God. However, in each instance, Bertocci notes qualifications that all but admit the personalistic thesis, viz., Xenophanes does admit that thought is the nature of ultimate being; Spinoza also admits that thought, as well as extension, defines the essence of substance;

and, Tillich speaks of the God who is the Personal—Itself—ground and abyss of every person.

Bertocci believes he can identify the cause of the continuing argument and offer a reasonable solution. "The storm that has raged around this concept has been caused by the 'model' that controlled the use of the word 'person'." Opponents of personalism rest their arguments on the assumption that a person can be defined as a social-biological phenomenon. "For the personalist, however, the word 'person' identifies an agent capable of self-consciousness and of action in the light of rational and moral-aesthetic-religious ideals."[13] Clearly this definition contains terms drawn from human experience which may be called anthropomorphisms, but Bertocci insists that such mental and spiritual activities may be legitimately applied to a model of the deity in ways that biological categories, like being "black" and having "blue eyes," cannot. Thus does he make a distinction between legitimate and illegitimate anthropomorphisms.

On a par with the notion that God as knower is a Person is the personalist's contention that God is a loving agent. This conclusion is empirically grounded in the datum of our human experience that love enhances all other values and is the key to reaching the highest and best in the universe. No deity short of a purposeful, loving Person could reasonably be thought to be ground of this kind of experience. Furthermore, there are definite requirements for this kind of self-realization which we do not invent and promulgate but which we find as a given in our universe. Specifically, we must become members of a "community of mutual concern." To love, that is, to live and grow as a "responsive-responsible" member of such a community is our highest good. The God who creates and sustains this kind of experience and this kind of order can be no less than the good and loving Person.[14]

We have found in the data gathered from biblical theism this same concept of God as good and loving Person. We might also include data from the modified Vedantas of Ramanuja and Madhva, though as we have seen there is a serious question as to whether Vishistadvaita is genuinely personalistic. The mention of Vedanta in the context of our discussion of love reminds us that Shankara seems to give the intellectual value of truth priority over the value of love. The goal of Vedanta is to come to awareness of

147

the truth experienced as *satchitananda,* whereas theism proclaims the great goal to be to love God and one's neighbors in response to being first loved by the God who is love. With respect to which value is more basic, Bertocci offers an imaginative insight. He contends that our search for knowledge is encouraged and sustained by love. Our world is such that it demands "mutual concern for the growth of persons as investigators who find and express themselves in sharing of insights."[15] Truth seeking also requires that we be free from the threat of persecution when our discoveries threaten the status quo. It would seem that Bertocci, reflecting the tradition of biblical theism, regards freedom and its fullest expression in love basic to the discovery of truth and all the other mutually sustaining and challenging values in human experience. This organization of values he regards as an "unfinished symphony" that requires creative orchestration within the individual and society and in relation to God; a growing system of values articulates the meaning of love as the creative purpose of humanity and God.

The fundamental theistic notion that God is personal love prepares the way for answering Heidegger's question, Why is there something rather than nothing? There are three possible ways in which "something"—or a world—could exist or not exist. (1) A world like ours could exist. (2) There might be no world at all. (3) There could be a world quite different from the one we know. Let us introduce Bertocci's definition of love. "When a person dedicates himself to the growth of other persons in full awareness of their mutual potential for growth, we say that he loves."[16] There is implicit here the underlying respect, concern, and care which persons who love feel for one another. Now if we accept our loving-God premise, we cannot imagine such a God willing an eternity devoid of all opportunity to actualize the love that defines his most basic attribute, because that would amount to a psychological, if not a logical, contradiction. It is part of the nature of love to share the best one has with the beloved. The creation of a world like ours in which values are potentially possible and where persons hunger for and are capable of realizing and actualizing these values is certainly compatible with the concept of sharing and caring love. There is "something rather than nothing"—the world as we know it—because God is a loving Person. We have really also dealt with the third possibility because a world quite different from what we know presumably would be so alien as to exclude what persons recognize as experiences of instrumental and intrinsic values and would be incompatible with our major premise of a loving God.

But to answer Heidegger's question by answering that divine love requires a world with persons opens the gate to the more difficult problem of the one and the many. To put it succinctly: How is God related to the world of nature and finite persons? If the great strength of the spiritual monisms is the unambiguous assertion that ultimate reality is One, the weakness of personalistic theism seems to be that it stumbles on the rocks of metaphysical pluralism in asserting that the real God created a real world with real persons.

In turning once again to Dr. Bertocci's analysis, we are very interested to see that in the course of discussing this topic, he actually becomes involved in doing the philosophy of comparative religion as he compares and contrasts the views of traditional theistic creationism with Advaita and Vishistadvaita. Drawing upon the thought of the Vedantin philosopher T. M. P. Mahadevan, Bertocci expresses the Vedantist objection to creationism as twofold. First, while recognizing that pluralism is untenable because two or more interacting forces require a third, and primal, force to explain their existence and their reciprocal behavior, creationism nevertheless falls into the same dilemma by positing real entities that are ontologically independent of God. Second, creationism means that for an inestimable period of time, God existed without the universe and finite persons. In short, the perfect deity was incomplete, unfulfilled, and in need—a logical contradiction if there ever was one.

Bertocci believes that the first objection can be answered if we understand the Creator-God as immanent in as well as transcendent to the world of nature and persons. In other words, the creation does not enjoy complete autonomy as in the case with traditional dualisms and pluralisms. The theist can assert that the space-time cosmos and finite persons are real while admitting that their very existence and their continuing interaction at all levels is wholly dependent on the one Creator-God, that is, dependent in ways consistent with personal finite freedom, about which we shall have more to say in the next chapter.

The second criticism poses the more difficult problem. Here the focus is not on the one and the many but on time and eternity. If we ascribe reality to time, it would seem that the Absolute will be subject to temporal forces in a way that would detract from self-sufficient perfection. As Mahadevan noted, God must be without his world in the time before creation and, again, persons freely acting in time will introduce new content into the divine experience. Vedantins and other monists agree that this is an intolerable and unacceptable model of the absolute being. They suggest that the solution is to reject *creatio ex nihilo* and realize that time is undergirded by eternity. Using Shankara's example of the rope that is mistaken for a snake, they explain that time exists but is not real. To claim that time is real is to make the same kind of a mistake as made by the one who calls the rope a real snake. Time is just another form of *maya* whose purpose it is to lead us to a deeper appreciation of the real. Thus saved out of the flux of the temporal process, the Absolute is eternally protected from any kind of want, all novelty and surprise. Brahma's perfection is beyond challenging.

Dr. Bertocci answers for personalism when he observes that the attempt to explain our experience of the temporal order as *maya* or *avidya* simply does not help us give an account of what we, as persons, really experience. Moreover, if we can never really know the Absolute as it is, how can we have confidence in the monist description of reality as beyond all time and distinctions?

We earlier recognized Ramanuja's attempt at a philosophical synthesis that would retain the traditional monist view of the Absolute above and beyond time and change and also the reality of the ordinary experience of the world of nature and persons. He sought to save the moral freedom of the individual person and the changeless perfection of the Absolute. The way he does this is to assert that "the world of distinctions is not due to *maya,* but, far from being independent of, actually constitutes the body of God, who includes it within his transcendent Unity."[17] But Bertocci sees what we also noticed in our earlier discussion of Vishistadvaita, namely, that there seems to be equivocation concerning the notion of finite beings. The Vishistadvaitins insist there is nothing wrong with saying that the finite self is both a substantial mode of Brahma and, at the same time, a unique, individual self. Brahma is at once the Unified Self and the soul of every finite person. In Bertocci's words, "We must simply confess that our own lack of insight, no doubt, makes it impossible for us to treat such statements as more than a juxtaposition of ideas."[18] Specifially, how can individual persons be focuses of the Ultimate and also be free and independent? How can the infinite be the ground of a world in which "something radically new, some novelty, not intrinsic to the meaning of Infinite (in the sense of completeness) is involved?" Bertocci concludes that neither Advaita nor Vishistadvaita adequately "corner the mystery" of the relation between God and the world and finite persons.

He turns to the theistic idea of *creatio ex nihilo* for the best answer. Regarding the "sheer novelty" that emerges in the world, he believes that the idea of creation deals with it most effectively. The theist must admit to the unsolved problem of the "how" of creation which might better be called "the mystery of coming into being." "But the doctrine of a Creator who transcends and yet sustains, preserves, and yet guides (consistent with free will), the finite persons he has created, does 'save' both the Infinite and the finite persons, and it does allow for interaction at many levels of intimacy."[19]

Dr. Bertocci's penetrating analysis has surely broken new ground in the doing of comparative philosophy; at least in dealing with certain expressions of Indian thought and Western theism. However, if we recall our evaluation of Vedanta, we will be reminded that there are three interpretations, and it is the last school, developed by Madhva, called Dvaita Vedanta, and not included in Dr. Bertocci's analysis, which might provide us with additional relevant insights. We recall that Madhva insisted on the unambiguous reality of differences in the space-time universe. Difference is the very basis for our knowing, and even to deny this is to demonstrate its truth because a denial refers to a different notion of what is believed to be correct. The relevant ideas of Dvaita are that Brahma, though ground of and immanent in the universe, is completely other than the world of nature and finite persons. The imperfection and suffering in the world of nature and persons makes it plain that Brahma cannot be equated with the world. There are three substances: things, selves, and Brahma. This solution attempts to save the perfection of the Absolute and the reality and independence of things and persons, as does Vishistadvaita, but it avoids stretching the meaning of language as we saw was the case with Ramanuja's synthesis. It may be, however, that we are once again confronting the old problem of pluralism as the name *Dvaita* suggests. Professor Koller asks: "But if these are maintained to be different substances it is hard to see how things and selves—as ultimate substances—could be dependent upon a third substance, for a substance is complete in itself and independent."[20]

It seems reasonable, in the light of the prevailing monistic tradition of Indian thought, that Madhva had no intention of suggesting any kind of ultimate pluralism. Koller's literal interpretation of the word *substance* must be softened to mean a dependent substance which, somehow, owes its existence to Brahma. It is precisely at this point that we are driven to postulate some kind of emanation or creation. Though we have come close to the creationist thesis, it is more likely that Madhva entertained the notion that the richness of the natural world with its finite persons is probably more reasonably accounted for as emanating from Brahma rather than as the product of *creatio ex nihilo.* In any case, it seems that we have in Dvaita Vedanta a genuine model of temporalistic personalism which, though avoiding *creatio ex nihilo,* offers thoughtful suggestions to explain the relationship between God, persons, and nature.

In concluding this section, we turn again to Dr. Bertocci in order to present what may be his most original contribution to personalistic theism. He recognizes that all three participants—creationists, Advaitins, and Vishistadvaitins (and he would probably agree to include Dvaitins)—make one unquestioned assumption, namely, that the eternal perfection of the Absolute, however related to the temporal worldly process, must never be conceived as being "infected by its imperfections." This assumption involves us in such difficulties that it must be questioned: "Why not," Bertocci asks, "reconceive the perfection of God so that good and evil, truth and error, progress and decay, can affect the qualitative manner in which God experiences himself and the world, and in a way consistent with his omnitemporal unity and continuity?"[21]

Bertocci finds the key to the traditional eternalistic theistic view of

God as perfect and unchanging Absolute in the doubtful notion that even our finite personal experience of succession is possible because of a "permanent underlying soul-substance." The bad model of the microcosm becomes the bad model of the macrocosm. Bertocci suggests that we jettison the idea of underlying soul substance—the soul-thread holding the beads of experience—as unnecessary baggage. "We actually experience ourselves as dynamic activities—in-unity. . . . Instead of being non-temporal, the 'I' is omnitemporal. . . . 'I' is not a collection of experiential items, but a unity of varied activities."[22]

This dynamic model of complex-unity-in-continuity, drawn from the actual experience of the finite person, provides us with a better model for the universal being than the eternalistic one. We now have an Omnitemporal Creator. Of course, the idea of perfection no longer means completeness but rather purposed growth and creativity in value experience in the responsive-responsible community that is rooted in and respects nature as the manifestations impersonal (not nonpersonal) of God's will. "God, on this view, would be the Creator-Sufferer-Lover, persuading, in many ways, finite persons to enter, as completely as their natures allow, into the tragic-joys of compassionate creativity."[23]

Concluding Observations

We have suggested that the philosophy of comparative religion provides the proper context for asking the question, What is the nature of ultimate reality? We began by referring to the provisional model developed by using empirical data supplied by the great religious philosophies. Our procedure involved an intensive analysis of the concepts suggested by this earlier work, ranging from nonpersonal to personal interpretations. Using philosophical categories of analysis and asking philosophical and religious questions, we probed each model to locate and distinguish the reasonable and probable from the untenable. In each case we found both strengths and weaknesses which need not be summarized here.

Aside from gaining a much more precise and detailed understanding of the merits and difficulties inherent in the several traditions, probably the most important value stemming from our work was to confirm the essential accuracy of our statements about the provisional model. Symbolically, we sketched out the boundaries of our model as propositions alpha and omega, representing the nonpersonal and personal parameters. We next identified corollaries that followed from these premises in terms of a spectrum of human experiences ranging from the nonrational-aesthetic to the rational-ethical. There appear to be no good reasons for abandoning this perspective. However, in the light of our analysis, we may, perhaps, sharpen some observations and include a diagram of the several models.

Dr. Bertocci's arguments for a model of God that is personal seem very strong, especially with regard to God as knower and loving agent. Other observations we made in the course of our analysis support his views, especially our points about free and ethically responsible persons in a cosmos that supports their striving for self-realization. All this strongly reinforces our "proposition omega" that God, or ultimate reality, must be a Person and not just personal or the ground of personal existence. One might even claim good reason for reversing our proposition, placing omega before alpha, but we will let the original order stand for the reason that Ultimate Being as infinite potential and source of all being is a broader and more inclusive concept which can involve the idea of God as Person, while to begin with the idea of a personal God would require such a number of qualifications and exceptions as to be awkward. We have discovered no reason to amend our corollaries, which have, if anything, been strengthened by our arguments—in this and the preceding section. However, in the next problem, dealing with the nature of persons, we hope to throw additional light on the correctness of their formulation.

ULTIMATE REALITY IS:

COSMIC PERSON

GOD
Creating

Real World

Real Persons

Real Time-Meaningful History

IMPERSONAL POWER

Purusha-Jiva-Yang

Prakriti-Ajiva-Yin

Eternal Cycling of the Process Universe

CONSCIOUS SPIRIT

Natural World

Community of Persons

Brahman as Narayana

World & Persons are Modes of Brahman

Nature

Persons

TAO

INFINITE POTENTIAL
Ground & Destiny of all Being

BASIC MODELS OF ULTIMATE REALITY

Chapter Seven:
The Nature and Destiny
of the Person

The question, What is the ontological status of the individual person? may very well be the most significant of the three special problems we are considering. Admittedly, questions about ultimate reality are of fundamental importance since any philosophical system must rest upon a metaphysical ground and axiological questions must receive satisfactory answers if any sense is to be made of the realm of value experiences, which alone make life worth living. But from the existential perspective and, indeed, from the point of view of epistemology, the individual person stands at the center of the inquiry. It is the individual person who experiences his or her existence with all its values and disvalues, asks questions about meaning, and seeks to discern the differences between truth and mere appearance. Conventional philosophy of religion, assuming the premises of Western theism about the reality of the finite person, has not dealt with the questions about the ontological status of the individual person in a sustained, systematic way. But because the philosophy of comparative religion recognizes a number of conflicting premises about the self, we must develop a complete analysis of this problem.

Our analysis of the nature of ultimate reality in terms of a continuum of concepts can also be applied to the present analysis. Let us imagine another continuum inclusive of all the possibilities regarding the nature of the self, ranging from a denial of the ultimate reality of finite persons through the affirmation of their ontological status as Cosmic Self to the view of their finite individual reality.

Advaita: Finite Persons Are Illusions

Advaita Vedanta, for all its seeming mysticism, is based squarely upon the triadic logical laws: an existing thing is what it is; it is not what it is and simultaneously not that; and it must be either one or the other case. Specifically, when the principle of noncontradiction is applied to the problem of the individual person, the conclusion is reached that the sense of the reality of our individual self must be illusory. This is because the metaphysical assumption that the One Brahman is the ultimate real category is the major premise from which it logically follows that this One cannot at the same time be many. Clearly, our existential perception regarding our ontological status must be some kind of an illusion. This, of course, is also the case regarding the rest of the phenomenal universe and, as we have seen, is identified by the term *maya*. There is no denying that Shankara's version of Vedanta offers an explanation of selfhood that is extremely powerful because of its simplicity, directness, and logical integrity. If intellectual excellence is to be defined as seeking meaning through unification, the progressive integration and reduction of a plethora of puzzling data to a reasonable, integrated pattern, then Advaita Vedanta must qualify as the finest flower in the realm of religious philosophy.

To further detail the point, we should note that in addition to the metaphysical solution, Advaita neatly solves epistemological and axiological problems as well. In the case of the former, by substituting epistemic monism for epistemic dualism it achieves perfect theoretic escape from the possibility of error since knowledge by identity is infallible and avoids the possibility of the distortion that must always accompany knowledge by acquaintance. By asserting that existential persons are really only facets of the One Person, it becomes theoretically possible to promise perfect knowledge to all, since "all" are really the One who possesses perfect knowledge of everything.

157

Regarding axiology, the problem of unifying our experiences of value is resolved by affirming a hierarchy of values, or perhaps the figure of concentric circles would be more helpful, with the ethical and religious values in the largest outer circle, appreciation of the aesthetic next, and intellectual values at the very center. Here, again, experiences of individual selfhood have only instrumental value in serving to lead us to the one intrinsic value: Atman, which is Brahman's Cosmic Self. We achieve this in the field of value experience as we move progressively from the perimeter of religious, ethical living, through aesthetic appreciation of the tumultuous phenomenal world to unity of individual self, *atman* or *jiva,* with Cosmic Self, Atman, where the final eternal experience is *satchitananda,* or blissful cosmic consciousness of true being. We acknowledge these positive features of Advaita but must also suggest that serious problems accompany these proffered solutions.

There is in the Western philosophical tradition a view regarding the essential worth of individual persons which finds classic expression in one of Kant's three formulations of the categorical imperative, that is, we must never use another person merely as a means to an end but always treat other persons as ends in themselves. It is at this point that Advaita seems to violate both intuition and reason. We should recall that Kant, like Shankara, assumed that the logical law is the ultimate measure of reasonable thinking and that the principle of humanity can be defended on logical grounds. Persons ought to be respected as beings of intrinsic worth because they alone possess the ability to reflect self-consciously and think rationally.

Now, the Advaita contention that our experience of individual selfhood is an illusion having only instrumental value clearly violates the principle of humanity. The Vedantin might well respond by saying that there is no intention to demean persons but, rather, to provide the way to genuine self-actualization. But the objection still remains that individual persons have no final worth in themselves, and it must be admitted that they are indeed being used to serve a higher goal, which can be achieved only by the sacrifice of the illusion of finite selfhood. There is another serious philosophical problem associated with this loss of finite selves that will be discussed later in the analysis.

The charge was made that Advaita seems also to violate our intuition. From ancient times, the existentialist insight regarding the psychological certainty individuals have about their existence and continuing identity has received serious attention. Augustine recognizes and discusses the phenomenon of certainty regarding self-knowledge with his formula *si fallor, sum* (If I am deceived, I exist), and Descartes' discussion of *cogito* is well known to students of philosophy. *Cogito ergo sum* (I think therefore I am), because to deny my individual existence requires my existence as the one who denies it. More recently, personalistic idealists like E. S. Brightman and Dr. Peter A. Bertocci have elaborated upon this concept. Professor Bertocci makes the point that the assertion "I exist" is both a perfect rational circle and intuitively certain. It is for personalism the sine qua non.[1]

The Advaitin, of course, answers that there is indeed both intuitive and rational certainty regarding the existence of the self.[2] However, the issue is not only the existence but the nature of the self which in Western personalistic assertions has a special meaning. No one using ordinary language means by "I" anything other than a finite personal self. Certainly, in the Western tradition we do not mean a cosmic soul or deity. When we make the leap from finite "I" to cosmic "I" does it not involve a Gestalt switch so enormous as to qualify as a "category mistake"? The original point seems to stand, that is the claim that individual persons are illusory violates ordinary intuition.

Regarding the destiny of the person, Advaita offers the imaginative notion of reincarnation as a facet of *samsara.* Often it is referred to as the endless succession of rebirths or the "wheel of birth and death." Curiously, unlike the Western hope to achieve immortality, the Eastern hope is to "get off the wheel" and achieve the bliss of *nirvana*—the passionless peace of *satchitananda.* The destiny of each soul is to work out its own salvation through countless rebirths. The cosmic principle of *karma,* the "law of the deed" which deals out justice, functions so that everyone is reborn into the most suitable circumstances in accordance with the merit and demerit earned in previous lives. Seemingly, we have here a schema that recognizes the value and potential of every person and provides for ultimate self-realization for all.

Now we have already commented on the problems associated

with confusing finite persons with the Cosmic Self, but quite apart from that issue, it seems that the concept of reincarnation also faces serious difficulties. To put it plainly, do we really have here a plan for the development of the self that respects the integrity and unique value of the person? We are told by Advaitins that we are on the path to experiencing our divine selfhood. But this is knowledge based on authority. What kind of knowledge do we have that is grounded in our experience? To have some degree of certainty regarding the direction or rate of our progress we would need to be able to compare our present state with our previous one(s). Otherwise, we can only conjecture. After all, we may be enjoying a pleasant, virtuous life, but it may not be as noble as the past one, if, indeed, there was a past one! The fact of the matter is that very few of us can recall past lives, and in the absence of such memory we have no way of measuring our progress or decline or even of knowing *why* we suffer or enjoy. Here, it would seem, is an especially important weakness in the doctrine. To grow as a person, intellectually, ethically, or in any way at all, requires that we profit from past experience. This certainly must be part of the definition of learning. In the absence of memories of past lives, our experience and learning must be limited to this present life. In effect, our past lives really have no pragmatic value whatsoever.

Now it is said by Advaitins that we really do have such knowledge of the past but that it is buried deep in our subconscious. This notion of material beyond or conscious awareness that nevertheless enters into our ethical choices seems to be rather like the problem of whether we can hold a person responsible for his actions if he was in fact predetermined or programmed to perform as he did. Let us recall another one of Kant's formulations of the categorical imperative. The principle of autonomy asserts that freedom lies at the very heart of the moral life and that ideally, persons freely adopt the moral law, as it cannot be imposed upon them. Furthermore, only actions that are freely performed from a sense of the rational ought have any moral worth. Subconscious drives appear to be very real, but we have no clear or unambiguous data to corroborate the Advaitins' contention that they derive from previous lives, and certainly such subconscious forces have no ethical status until they emerge into our conscious awareness and are selected or rejected as a function of our freedom of choice. We must conclude that alleged subconscious residue of previous lives does not offer a very persuasive argument for either the truth or usefulness of reincarnation.

There remains another objection to this doctrine, and it may be the most fundamental. Let us begin by asking just what it is that is most striking about our awareness of our self-identity. Clearly, there is the immediate phenomenon of self-consciousness as distinct from mere animal consciousness. I know that I am, can reflect upon it and articulate it to myself and to others. But if such reflection is to be more than an instantaneous, perishable point-event in my psyche, I must remember it and be able to recall it all along the continuum of my personal experience, which I call my memory. Indeed, it seems that the basic ingredient in personal experience is the ability to recall myself at T-1, T-2, T-3, etc. My personal history is basic to my being me, and if I have lived innumerable lives which are beyond my recall, then in what sense can it be said that I really lived them? Wouldn't it be as if I should awake each morning with amnesia—with no knowledge of the preceding day? To be sure, there would be a sense in which it could be said that, objectively, I was the same person, but, subjectively, would this be true? Would it be meaningful? This amnesia phenomenon raises serious doubts about the truth of the theory of reincarnation.

The doctrine of reincarnation is an imaginative concept that tries to make sense of life and conserve the dignity and value of the person, but our objections seem to have revealed that it has serious weaknesses. The destiny of Brahman is secure but not the destiny of finite persons.

Theravada Buddhism: The Soul Is an Epiphenomenon

Adjacent to the Advaita Vedantist position on our continuum is that of Buddhism, which devotes even more energy to an intensive analysis of the mystery of the self. The conclusion reached is very similar to that of Advaita: the eperience of finite selfhood is based upon an illusion founded on ignorance of the true state of affairs. The finite self does not exist; at least, it is not the autonomous entity we suppose it to be. But whereas Advaita reaches its conclusion by beginning with a demanding monistic metaphysics developed in terms of a rigorous application of the principle of noncontradiction,

Buddhism begins with the premise of a process philosophy, which is then developed along the lines of physiological psychology.

Early Theravada Buddhism proclaimed a radical process view of reality in the phrase *Yat sat tat ksanikam* (All things are as brief as winks), which is known as the doctrine of the flux. Eternal processes of matter-energy seem to be metaphysical ground here, and cosmology is developed in terms of a kind of emergent evolution with the conscious, finite self the latest emergent. Unlike modern Western naturalism, however, the status of reality is not conferred upon this emergent. Indeed, the Buddhist doctrine of *anatta,* or *anatman,* specifically denies that the *atman,* or personal self, is real. It is only a temporary composite phenomenon, fully comprehensible only in terms of the "wheel of becoming" whereby we understand that the entire universe conspires to produce the multitudinous illusions of finite selves as innumerable physical forces and phenomena interact with psychic and social forces to create this complex force field. As "quick as a wink," each momentary self is born, experiences, and perishes, so that only the existential moment is real. There is no persisting self or soul to give continuity but only the similarity of each successive self with its former self, which creates an illusion of substantial selfhood. The individual self is really an epiphenomenon.

This notion of process is carefully expounded by the Buddhist doctrine of *pratityasamutpada,* or the theory of dependent origination. The formula "This being, that arises" develops the idea that everything in the empirical realm is relative, conditional, dependent, and impermanent. In looking for a parallel in Western philosophy we probably come close when we match *pratityasa-mutpada* with epiphenomenalism, the theory that mind is a dependent and only temporary phenomenon produced by the phenomenon of the physical brain.[3]

This radical process view of reality is nicely complimented with Buddhist psychology, which begins by recognizing that suffering is inherent in living because of desires impossible of fulfillment, the chief ones being desire to escape sickness, old age, and death. Since it is the self that entertains these hopeless desires, the only way to escape constant anxiety and torment is to lose the self. Buddhist process metaphysics has provided the answer—there is no real self, so the self's desires must also be illusory. Freed from the desires, because we are no longer ignorant about the true nature of ourself, we are released from suffering and *nirvana* is ours!

This view of the nonreality of the self propounded by Theravada Buddhism is without peer in nihilist philosophy. From a pragmatic view it might be judged as effective in obtaining its goal of passionless peace, but the price it pays is quite unacceptable if we take seriously the potential of the person for self-realization. Any philosophy that seriously advances such a negative view of the self must itself be regarded negatively on the basis of our earlier point that denying the reality of the finite self goes against both reason and intuition. At least in Advaita, the finite person served in an instrumental capacity; here in Theravada it serves none. The universe must be regarded as truly absurd, but such a conclusion is just not compatible with the tentative model we have constructed. It fails to take into account much significant data, especially those important value claims that rest upon the capacity of the person to experience the truth, beauty, goodness, and holiness. All would be quite meaningless, indeed, impossible, without a substantial self to entertain those experiences of value.

Mahayana Buddhism:
The Finite Self is a Projection of Cosmic Buddha

Mahayana Buddhism adopts but adapts the doctrine of the flux to its idealistic metaphysics. Its monistic idealism closely parallels that of Vedanta, as we have noted, and the Mahayana view of the finite personal self as a temporary plane of experience on the way to realization of unity with the Cosmic Buddha Mind, or Dharmakaya, is very close to the view advanced by Advaita. However, there is an important innovation in the matter of axiology. Where Advaita seems to put the intellectual truth value at the center, the Buddhist ethics and especially the life of the Bodhisattva is characterized by this compassion toward all sentient beings. This emphasis on altruism makes the Buddhist model of the self immediately attractive.

But this approval is almost at once dispelled when we reflect that as in the cast of Advaita, the finite selves have no ontological status. How can *ahimsa* compassion, however strikingly portrayed, have any permanent value when in eternity only the One Cosmic

Buddha Self exists? Altruism in this setting must dissolve into egoism, or to put it plainly, all the love offered to others is finally offered to one's own self! Mahayana appears to have run into a terrible paradox, namely, if we declare finite selves to be illusory, then the altruism they manifest to one another must also be illusory. When the chief value of a philosophy is lost, what is left to recommend the philosophy? Nonetheless, Mahayana's concept of ideal persons who love other persons and are sensitive to the suffering of all sentient creatures, even the lowliest, to the point of sacrificing themselves, is unparalleled in the religious literature of the world and must find a suitable expression in a mature philosophy of comparative religion. But the same objections we found with the Vedanta view of persons must also apply to Mahayana. Reason and intuition demand more for persons than to declare them to be finally unreal or worthy of only instrumental service in the attainment of a higher goal.

Tao Hsueh:
Persons are Temporary Manifestations of Tao

Later Taoism appears to owe much to Mahayana Buddhism with respect to metaphysics and the idea of the personal self.[4] Tao takes the place of Dharmakaya, and the Buddhist idea of eternal process is incorporated into the ancient Chinese intuition that "reversal is the way of the Tao." But regarding the status of the individual person, a more natural, relaxed attitude is taken. Persons seem to be accepted as real, and no elaborate scenario is developed to explain them away either as illusion or instant atomic winks. Persons with all their emotions, potential for creativity, and experiences of value are real, at least for the time of their brief passage as part of the eternal flux; then they seem to contribute their energy to the mysterious Tao source from which they emerged. Any hoped-for continuing sense of identity and experience after death is vain. Persons must achieve whatever degree of self-actualization is possible within the brief span between birth and death. This is guided by the ethics of *Ju chia* that is incorporated into Tao Hsueh, as we have already noted.

It would seem that Tao Hsueh has a view of persons that recognizes their intrinsic worth and avoids the criticism leveled at Advaita and Mahayana with respect to treating persons merely as means. Even human altruism, *jen* love, retains its identity instead of suffering an ignoble reduction to egoism. Nor are persons urged to disavow their sense of really existing and accept the absurdity of the universe as with Theradavada. The Chinese views here identified recognize the worth of persons and are specially sensitive to the role of artistic creativity and the aesthetic experience in nurturing mature personhood. But it is all over for each of us at death, and beyond the comparatively brief time of frenetic striving here on earth there seems to be no overarching telos for humankind or for the Tao itself. Such a view of persons seems truncated in view of its inability to account for and provide for developing the human potential so often frustrated by inequities and quirks of fate.

Kant readily admitted that the notion of personal immortality is beyond rational proof in the *Critique of Pure Reason,* but in his *Critique of Practical Reason,* he just as forcefully argues that personal immortality is the only reasonable conclusion for beings who experience the moral ought of the categorical imperative. Of course, Kant was presuming a rational ground of the cosmos which could not demand a perfect moral life apart from providing continuing opportunity for growth toward the ideal and redress of grievances without violating the laws of reason. That the concept of Tao includes no such rigorous logical presumption would explain the Chinese view of persons, but it also raises questions about the adequacy of Taoist metaphysics in the light of important existential and ethical claims associated with persons. We will consider the ethical experience of persons respecting the matter of immortality later in the analysis. For the present, we observe that Taoism seems to have offered a view of persons that at least advances us along the continuum in the direction of a more substantial concept of the reality of finite persons having worth in their own right.

Vishistadvaita:
Persons are Poises of Being of Narayana

Vishistadvaita Vedanta is next on our continuum of models of the person, and here we seem to encounter for the first time the notion that finite persons are both real and immortal. Ramanuja argues, as we have noted, that if Narayana, or Supreme Person (Ramanuja's preferred) name for Brahman is real, then all he creates must also be just as real. Hence, the cosmos, or nature, and finite persons must be real and not *maya.* For persons, the purpose of existence is to progress by practicing yoga to the highest self-attainment possible, individually and collectively, until each self knows itself to be a "poise of being for Brahma." The resulting perfect society which Radhakrishna calls the *brahmaloka,* or kingdom of Brahma, will be characterized by the "holy calm, supreme self-mastery and righteous action" of the saints.[5] In Aurobindo's interpretation, the spiritual kingdom within will be transformed by spiritual evolution into a radically different earth-life and earth-nature in which the gnostic beings enjoy complete harmonious living with one another and with nature.[6]

These views of Vedanta seem to have avoided the weakness of Advaita while preserving the virtues of Vedanta metaphysics. But when we consider the word *Vishistadvaita,* we recognize that it means qualified nondualism, or positively, qualified monism. To explicate the point, consider Vishistadvaita in a triune perspective, that is, there are three eternal modes of Brahman: (1) Brahma, or God the eternal ground of all being; (2) nature, or God externally expressing himself in the space-time cosmos, biological evolution, etc.; (3) persons, or God eternally revealing himself in finite spirits.

If we are to take the noun *advaita* (monism) seriously, then, whatever the qualifications suggested by the adjective *vishis,* Brahman remains just as much the only One as in Advaita. As we noted earlier, there is only an apparent distinction between God, nature, and persons; finally, all is really part of the One, including finite selves. The qualified monist might explain, "Yes, but individual persons do have intrinsic worth and they retain their distinctive individuality even in their perfected state." To which we must reply: Perhaps, but the individuality they retain is a "poise of being for Brahma" and not ontological reality. Persons seem to be rather like self-conscious limbs and sense organs doing the bidding of the conscious person who commands and coordinates the body rather than true autonomous beings in their own right.[7] Vishistadvaita may have avoided conflict with the principle of humanity, but it still violates ordinary intuition regarding self-exis-tence and identity and encounters the same problem as Mahayana in that all altruism must become egoism because all loving service is really offered to oneself.

Dvaita:
Persons are Predestined Emmanations of Brahma

We recall the third interpretation of Vedanta, developed by Madhva in the thirteenth century C.E. and called Dvaita, that is, divided or dualistic Vedanta. More correctly, the term might be rendered "pluralistic idealism." Theory of knowledge provides the starting point for understanding Madhva's interpretation as he explains that to know something means to know that it is different from all other things. The essence of this pluralistic philosophy is expressed by the phrase "everything is unique." It is this concept that difference, *bheda,* is a "final fact" that differentiates Dvaita from the monistic interpretations of Vedanta.[8]

It follows, then, that the realms of nature and finite persons are "different" from Brahma, that is, they exist in their own right and actually can be said to have independent existence. Unlike the monisms, nature and persons are not part of God, or Brahman. But Dvaita is not pluralistic like the cosmic naturalisms in which each element or particle is ontologically real. Madhva explains that God alone is independently real. He brings nature and persons into being, and they are real because they are his creations that exist in space and time. However, unlike the monisms, all things and all persons are dependent upon God's *will* for their existence; they are not derived from his *being.* It is this distinction that gives us a model of persons that preserves the integrity of their individuality and thereby avoids the aforementioned difficulties.

There remains one more feature of this system, however, which raises a serious and perhaps insurmountable problem. It is the assertion that God is both all-loving and all-powerful, or as personalists would say, it is absolutistic theism. It does avoid the typical fundamentalist two-story, dualistic model of the universe—with almighty God hovering above the world and from time to time invading the realm of nature to perform supernatural miraculous deeds. Dvaita contends that God is immanent in the world and controls it from within, through what we perceive to be natural processes. This kind of control applies also to finite persons to the extent of involving predestination for the three basic categories, viz., those condemned eternally to hell, those who must recycle endlessly from life to life, and those who may evolve to eventual freedom. Determinism seems evident in every case,

167

including the last, in which freedom seems to mean self-understanding or freedom from ignorance rather than the ability to make existential choices in the realm of values.

Such a view of the person raises again the ancient dispute regarding the nature and significance of human freedom. Let us at once clarify that the meaning intended here is neither the empirical kind of freedom associated with political and civil liberties nor the theological variety expressed as deliverance from the bondage of sin but what we shall term *metaphysical freedom;* that is, to recognize the person as a self-conscious agent capable of choosing between two or more alternatives. By choice we mean a conscious selection which, though influenced by external factors of prior conditioning, environment, habit, chance, and set purpose, is not necessary either in the sense of logical entailment or physical coercion.

We earlier recalled the ancient point that ethical responsibility is incompatible with determinism, for how can one praise or condemn a foreordained agent? To imagine a robot with programmed circuits or a person in a posthypnotic state or under the influence of a powerful drug and consider how meaningful moral criticism would be is to answer the rhetorical question. Kant states the position very forcefully with the exclamation "If I ought, I can." Put another way, "ought" and "must" are quite incompatible as regards the ethical life. William James makes a similar observation, only he analyzes the feeling of "regret" rather than the experience of "ought."

Even more fundamental from a theoretical perspective is the relationship between thinking and freedom. To think reflectively, as distinguished from mere idle reverie involving stream-of-consciousness associations, is to make conscious choices about the direction the thinking will take and concerning conclusions, steps in a sorites, selection of data, etc. An unfree person can no more think responsibly and reach a meaningful conclusion than can a fixed jury reach an acceptable verdict. Both jury and thinker must be free from external coercion; free to peruse the relevant data and reach conclusions guided by the canons of logic. Borden Parker Bowne, the founder of personalistic idealism in the United States, asserted that freedom is the sine qua non of the intellectual life.[9] Bertocci later is to state that "true" and "false" would be just as meaningless, that is, beyond all possibility of arguing, as "right" and "wrong," without freedom. Kant's principle of autonomy, which states that all moral acts must be freely chosen, is grounded in his assumption that freedom is a necessary prerequisite of thinking persons.

Apart from metaphysical freedom there can be neither ethical nor intellectual life. Insofar as Dvaita Vedanta incorporates determinism in its view of persons, we find it inadequate. However, of all the systems studied so far, Dvaita alone offers a model of the finite person that incorporates enduring intrinsic value and an autonomous status compatible with the dignity we ideally associate with persons. Moreover, Dvaita emphasizes God's saving grace and the love between him and finite persons above intellectual attainment and avoids reducing altruism to egoism as in the other Vedantas and Mahayana. When we moved on to Dvaita Vedanta, we really came very close to the last category on our continuum: the biblical interpretation of personalistic theism. It remains for us to conclude this analysis with critical attention now directed toward the view of the person developed in Western biblical theism.

Biblical Theism: Persons Are Free Creations of God

Personalistic theism shares with Dvaita the idea that individual, finite persons are ontologically real and distinct from God and the rest of nature. The clear intuitive perceptions of self-existence and self-identity persisting through time and change are taken seriously and are the foundation of this model, which finds expression throughout biblical literature. One has only to sample stories from the Bible to recognize the radical difference from the ideas presented in other scriptures. Specifically, the biblical theme is developed within the framework of *Heilsgeschichte,* or holy history, in which the Person God creates and leads finite persons through countless experiences, primarily of an ethical and religious nature, for the purpose of achieving an interpersonal community of creative, ethical love. While the goal reminds us of the interpretations of Vedanta expressed by Radhakrishnan and Aurobindo, the very fact that in the biblical view, persons are not "poises of being" for the Absolute but in literal fact, real individuals, makes all the difference.

This difference has to do with the values that alone give meaning to existence. Earlier, we noted the difficulty with the Vedantin view that the imperfect and sometimes unethical notions of finite persons must also be those of Brahma. Such a concept runs afoul of the principle of noncontradiction and makes a shambles of the ideal value of objective truth. We have also commented on the inability of both Vedantin and Buddhist models to save the value of love from being swallowed up in a lofty cosmic egoism. It would seem that only a radical personalism that unequivocally asserts the ontological reality of finite persons can provide a firm foundation for these two values. Only if there are real, individual persons can we satisfactorily account for error while maintaining our ideal of objective truth, and only if there are real, individual persons can an "I" encounter and love a "thou" in the sense of outgoing concern and care for another. Indeed, it is this last point that lies at the heart of the biblical ethos, whether it be expressed as Yahweh's love for Israel at the Exodus of the Father's love for his children in the gift of his Son. This love—*hesed,* or *agape*—is an expression of deep concern and dramatic caring of One for others and cannot be reduced to self-love.

These two values, truth and love, come to be realized, or approximated, in the lives of individuals in the course of experiences that often depend upon decision making. The experience of making a choice is quite as basic to human experience as are the experiences of self-existence and self-identity. However, it must be admitted that intuitions of being driven by fate or powers beyond one's control are also numerous, and the biblical data are often ambiguous. On the one hand, we find numerous examples of divine laws and instructions given with the clear understanding that humans are free to obey or to disobey. Joshua reads the covenant to the people and concludes, "Choose this day whom you will serve." Ezekiel cries, "Turn . . . and get yourselves a new heart!" On the other side, we read that "Yahweh hardened the heart of Pharaoh" and apparently caused him to change his mind about letting the Hebrew slaves escape. In the Gospel of Matthew, we encounter the *testimonia,* passages that explain that such and such happened "in order that the scriptures might be fulfilled."

With such ambiguous and inconclusive scriptural evidence, theologians and philosophers down through the ages have taken opposing positions but sometimes sought to narrow the gap and even achieve an uneasy synthesis. Augustine recognizes both God's omnipotence and man's ethical accountability by making a distinction between foreordination and foreknowledge. In the realm of human responsibility, he can ascribe foreknowledge to God without robbing man of his freedom. D. M. Baillie can quote from Paul: "I worked harder than any of them, though it was not I, but the grace of God which is with me" (I Cor. 15:10*b*), and suggest that God is certainly no less free than we and can influence our choices without violating the freedom so essential to our humanity. Baillie explains: "It is what we may call the paradox of grace . . . for in ascribing it all to God it does not abrogate human personality nor disclaim personal responsibility."[10] Reinhold Niebuhr can say that "sin is inevitable, but not necessary," thereby making a nice distinction between empirical probability and logical entailment.

> The Christian doctrine of original sin with its seemingly contradictory assertions about the inevitability of sin and man's responsibility for sin is a dialectical truth which does justice to the fact that man's self-love and self-centeredness is inevitable, but not in such a way as to fit into the category of natural necessity. It is within and by his freedom that man sins.[11]

Clearly, a reasonable decision for freedom or determinism will have to rest on the philosophical analysis of the problem which we have already offered earlier in our discussion of Dvaita. We concluded that neither the moral nor the intellectual life would be possible without some degree of freedom. Our use of the word *decision* above dramatically reveals the intimate relationship between freedom and reflective thinking. If one of the positive features of the theistic model of the person is the place it affords to values, then certainly another is its insistence that persons enjoy a measure of finite freedom. It is this second point that sets it apart from the personalistic model of Dvaita and, as we have seen, makes the other values meaningful and attainable.

While the biblical models of God and finite individuals are personalistic, they are not identical. In the last chapter we reviewed the details of the nature of the divine Person; now, in focusing on the nature of the finite individual, we must take note of a critical difference. Quite simply, while the Person God is eternally self-existent, finite persons owe their existence to divine creation and come into being at a specific time. Unless we presuppose pre-existence, and the biblical tradition does not, and if we make a distinction between the material body with its inherited genes and the spirit, which we call the person, there seems to be no way around saying that persons are created *ex nihilo.* But the notion of *ex nihilo* has long been a kind of metaphysical thorn in the mind and is traditionally rebutted with the phrase *ex nihil, nihil fit* !

A more traditional naturalistic metaphysics would probably prefer to explain the occurrence of new persons as a kind of emergence triggered by a critical mass of matter-energy in the form of brain and nervous system. The trouble with this view is that it is vulnerable to reverse analysis that leads to reductionism and perhaps even to materialism. Then we are left with the problem of explaining how the potential for life, consciousness, and purpose got into matter in the first place.

An idealist metaphysics, of course, would explain that the qualities of mind or spirit have always constituted the very essence of what we call matter, so there is no need to smuggle it into natural man or call it forth magically, out of nothing.[12] But if theism is to avoid the all-swallowing monism of Vedanta and other monisms, it must, in order to save the ontological status of the person with all the values he represents, modify traditional absolute idealism and make two points clear. The temporal evolutionary process is real, and individual persons come into existence as part of the Spirit that nurtures all things but with conscious minds that possess genuine autonomy, much as children are a product of their parents but become truly independent individuals. The idea of genuine creation must be recognized, underscoring the idea that finite individuals do not exist before they are born into the world. The point is to avoid the absolutist idea of the eternal existence of persons which would compromise their dependent and individual status. Their dependence must be affirmed if we are to avoid pluralism, and their individual status must be affirmed if we would avoid the problems inherent in the absolute monisms relating to freedom, truth, and love that were earlier discussed. Brightman rightly grasps the problem and expresses it very clearly:

> If the soul is literally one with God in its very being, then man's responsibility and his moral life as a person are at an end. Only God is

responsible for God. To cancel moral endeavor is to cut the root of prophetic religion everywhere and to destroy the tie between religion and human character.[13]

Finally, the model of the person offered by personalistic theism comes to grips with the question about human destiny. Of the other models, only Dvaita allows that persons, perceived as genuine individuals, will survive biological death and move toward their destiny. But it was over the point of a predetermined destiny that we finally judged Dvaita to be of questionable value. Moreover, Dvaita, like the other systems of Vedanta, explains the afterlife, or rather afterliving, in terms of *samsara* cycles of rebirth on earth as well as in various heavens and hells, and we have earlier discussed the questionable features of that concept. It seems that only biblical theism conceives of an afterlife for real finite persons that would be a continuation of the striving after values begun in this earthly life. That is, unlike the *samsara* doctrine, which must recognize the amnesia phenomenon that we all experience regarding alleged previous lives, the biblical concept promises that our memories and sense of identity will remain intact. Of course, this well-developed, sophisticated concept is not to be found in the earliest biblical literature.

In pre-exilic Hebrew religion, the person enjoyed real existence only until biological death, which marked the end of life both physically and spiritually. Despite vague references to the shadowy realm of sheol, the place of the spirits of the dead, in those earliest times there seems to have been no clear-cut concept of immortality or life after death. The notion of resurrection of body and soul to face judgment and assignment to heaven or hell, we have seen, was borrowed from the proto-Persian religion of Zoroastrianism during the period of the Babylonian captivity. The idea of the continuing reality of the soul after death is refined and expressed in late Judaism, e.g., in the theology of the Pharisees, and later in the Christian faith.

The idea of immortal personhood has received considerable attention from philosophers from Plato to current speculation about the data provided by parapsychology. The most reasonable arguments seem to be those suggested by Kant and Brightman. Kant, we earlier noted, based his argument on the primacy of the ethical imperative, which demands a life of moral perfection quite

173

unlikely to be attained during our brief sojourn on planet Earth. Because persons may not merely be used but by virtue of their rational nature must be provided with opportunity to realize their moral potential, an ongoing life may be presumed as reasonable. Anything less would be not only cruel deception but a clear violation of the notion of rationality, which grounds Kant's world view. A modern version of this argument might point out that to seriously argue against this point, one would really have to subscribe to the premise advanced by some existentialists and Theravadins that the world is indeed absurd.

Brightman enlarges his argument to include all values that are really basic to his personalistic idealism. The argument turns on the word *axiology,* or value theory, really theory of worth. Only value, or worth, can provide reason for there being "something rather than nothing," but only persons can have experiences of value. Brightman distinguishes between "actual values" experienced by persons and "potential values" that provide a kind of raw material for personal experience. We might term this *objective relativism,* in which any value, e.g., truth, goodness, beauty, holiness, can emerge only in the mind of the sensitive person when he or she is in a particular relationship with objective reality. Since actual values exist only in the minds of persons, human and divine, a world without persons would be a world devoid of actual values or worth. Now it might be observed that since God is the cosmic Person, the world will have worth irrespective of the presence or absence of human or finite persons. Brightman, however, suggests moral laws of "the most inclusive ends" and "the best possible" which develop the notion that it is best to maximize experiences of value.[14] On the basis of this thesis, a world with a community of creative persons would be more desirable than a solitary deity, no matter how marvelous his omnipowers might be. The argument concludes that if God is the creator and conservator of values, then he must also conserve persons who are values in and of themselves and also experiencers of values. In terms of the conservation of values, immortality is seen to be a reasonable belief and hope.

This argument is strengthened by emphasizing that God's nature is most significantly defined in terms of his goodness and love. Where Kant appealed to the demand of reason to support his argument for personal immortality, Brightman follows more closely the biblical theme of *agape* love as highest value and contends that if God is like a good and loving parent, then he will provide for the continuing well-being of his children. Otherwise, God would be a cosmic monster who warms his hands at a fire fed by the endless succession of generations of his own children![15] For Brightman, it is this feature of divine goodness and love that provides the strongest argument for personal immortality, and we have considered the arguments regarding the divine nature in the preceding chapter.

We should recognize that these arguments for immortality all assume that persons have intrinsic worth and stand at the apex of a hierarchy of values. If they are conserved, it is not an arbitrary act but occurs because persons are worth saving or at least are potentially worthy. They are capable of growing and achieving increasingly higher levels of value experience which would include coherent integration of character and creative living.

Concluding Observations

All things considered, it would seem that the model of the person offered by personalistic theism has much to recommend it. It gives us a model that includes the created, ontological reality of finite, individual persons, allows for a degree of finite freedom so necessary for the development of the intellectual and moral dimensions of life, and provides for continuing experience and growth beyond biological death. We have identified several instances where one or more of these basic attributes was weak or impossible in the other models.

However, if this is a victory for this particular model of persons, it is a qualified one at best. In the course of our analysis we discovered features in the other models so positive and significant for the development of a truly comprehensive model of the person that we now know that the view of personalistic theism cannot stand alone. Appreciation for the aesthetic nature of humanity, the possibility of intimate union of mind and spirit with the One, the very present intimate relationship humans have with the complex force field called nature, are only a few priceless insights provided by Taoist, Vedantin, and Buddhist thought. All attempts to seriously investigate philosophical problems pertaining to persons must take into account the vital insights provided by Eastern thought.

175

Probably one of the most valuable lessons learned by our attempt to develop a philosophy of comparative religion is that no single religious philosophy holds a monopoly on the truth. In fact, truth appears to be multifaceted, that is, a state of affairs may be viewed, appreciated, and analyzed from a variety of perspectives. Certainly, our planetary perspective on religion has afforded a much more interesting view than is possible from any lesser frame of reference. It is to be hoped that our methodology, which has served us well in our limited analysis, will prove useful to others who will surely discover other equally interesting problems worthy of investigation.

PERSONS ARE

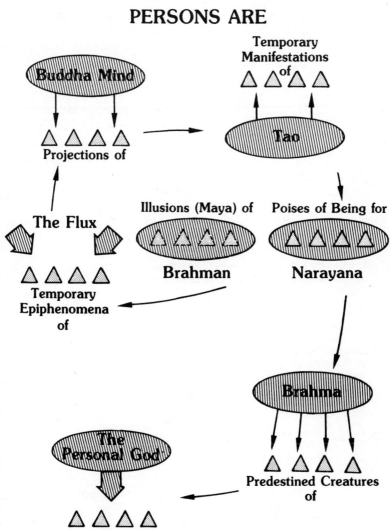

BASIC MODELS OF PERSONS

Notes

Chapter One

1. Albert Schweitzer, *Philosophy of Civilization* (New York: Macmillan, 1960), pp. 95, 109, 110, 110.
2. Ibid., p. 217.
3. Ibid., p. 241.
4. Ibid., pp. 301, 302, 303.
5. Ibid., pp. 305, 309, 305, 283, 309.
6. Rudolph Otto, *Mysticism East and West: A Comparative Analysis of the Nature of Mysticism,* trans. Bertha L. Bracey and Richenda C. Payne ([1932] New York: Macmillan, 1962), pp. 5, 6. In the preface, Otto explains that in this book he has "collected, completed, and expanded" the lectures he delivered at Oberlin College in the autumn of 1924.
7. Ibid., p. 47.
8. Ibid., p. 50.
9. Ibid., pp. 198, 204.
10. Ibid., pp. 198, 204.
11. Ibid., p. 223.
12. Ibid., p. 210.
13. Ibid., pp. 225, 223.
14. S. Radhakrishnan, *Eastern Religions and Western Thought,* 2nd ed. (New York: Oxford University Press, 1940), pp. 59, 306, viii, ix.
15. Ibid., p. 336.
16. Ibid., pp. 338.
17. Ibid., p. 331.
18. Ibid., p. 340.
19. Ibid., p. 340, quoted from Müller, *Introduction to Science of Religion,* p. 68.
20. Ibid., p. 341; p. 341, n. 1; p. 341, Barth as quoted in Macnicol, *Is Christianity Unique?* (1936), pp. 168-69.
21. Ibid., p. 344.
22. Ibid., p. 347.
23. Ibid.

24. W. E. Hocking, *The Coming World Civilization* (New York: Harper, 1956), pp. xiv, 136.
25. Ibid., p. 138.
26. Ibid., p. 139.
27. Ibid., p. 141.
28. Ibid., p. 149.
29. Ibid., pp. 153, 157-58.
30. Ibid., pp. 159, 161.
31. F. S. C. Northrop, *The Meeting of East and West* ([1946] New York: Macmillan 1960), p. ix.
32. Ibid., p. 294.
33. Ibid., pp. 295, 297, 299.
34. Ibid., pp. 315, 303.
35. Ibid., pp. 304, 316.
36. Ibid., pp. 319, 333, 334.
37. Ibid., pp. 304, 375-76.
38. P. T. Raju, *Introduction to Comparative Philosophy* (Lincoln: University of Nebraska Press, Arctures Books, 1970), p. 251.
39. Ibid., pp. vii, 3.
40. Ibid., pp. 283, 285, 292, 294, 297, 297.
41. Ibid., pp. 10-11.
42. Gerardus Van der Leeuw, *Religion in Essence and Manifestation: A Study in Phenomenology,* trans. G. E. Turner, p. 674, as quoted in B. L. Slater, *World Religions and World Community,* 2 vols. (New York: Columbia University Press, 1963). I:32.
43. Slater, *World Religions and World Community,* I:32.
44. Ibid., I:37.
45. Ibid., I:46.
46. Ibid., I:202, 227.
47. Ibid., I:201, 206, 213.
48. John Bowker, *Problems of Suffering in Religions of the World* (London: Cambridge University Press, 1970), p. 290.
49. Ibid., p. 283.
50. Ibid., pp. 20, 21.
51. John Hick, ed., *Truth and Dialogue in World Religions: Conflicting Truth Claims* (Philadelphia: Westminster Press, 1970), pp. 13, 15, 18.
52. Ibid., p. 58.
53. Ibid., p. 102.
54. Ibid., p. 101.
55. Ibid., p. 30.
56. Ibid., pp. 140, 142.
57. Ibid., pp. 147, 145-46.
58. Ibid., p. 148.
59. Ibid., pp. 149, 151.
60. Ibid., pp. 153, 154.
61. C. A. Moore, *Philosophy: East and West* (Freeport, N. Y.: Princeton University Press, Books for Libraries Press, Early Index Reprint Series, 1970), p. vii.
62. Mircea Eliade, *Patterns in Comparative Religion,* trans. Rosemary Sheed (New York: World Publishing, Meridian Books, 1966), p. xiv.
63. Joseph Campbell, *The Masks of God,* 2 vols. (New York: Viking Press, 1962), II:22.

64. Michael Pye, *Comparative Religion: An Introduction Through Source Materials* (New York: Harper, 1972), pp. 19, 20, 20.

Chapter Two

1. The moral dimension of the religious life is critically presented by P. A. Bertocci, *Introduction to Philosophy of Religion* (Englewood Cliffs, NJ: Prentice-Hall, 1958), and D. Elton Trueblood, *Philosophy of Religion* (New York: Harper and Brothers, 1957) introduces an aesthetic argument for God, pp. 118-30. *See also* Howard Hunter, ed., *Humanities, Religion and the Arts Tomorrow* (New York: Holt, Rinehart and Winston, 1971), p. 1.
2. Willem F. Zuurdeeg, *An Analytical Philosophy of Religion* (Nashville: Abingdon, 1958), p. 56.
3. Frederick Ferré, *Basic Modern Philosophy of Religion* (New York: Scribner's, 1967), pp. 342-45.
4. William G. Doty, *Contemporary New Testament Interpretation* (Englewood Cliffs, NJ: Prentice-Hall, 1972), p. 31.
5. Ibid., p. 43.
6. Fung Yu-Lan, *A Short History of Chinese Philosophy,* trans. Derk Bodde (New York: Macmillan, 1960), chs. 1, 2; pp. 1-29.
7. Mai-mai Sze, *The Way of Chinese Painting* (New York: Random, Vintage Books, 1959), pp. 430-31.
8. James Legge, *The Texts of Taoism,* 2 vols., Sacred Books of the East, ed. Max Müller ([1891] New York: Dover, 1962), Part 2: "The Writings of Kwan-Sze [Chuang Tzu]," pp. 57-58, 142-43. In this selection, Chuang Tzu discusses the metaphorical character of his language. *See also* Fung, *Chinese Philosophy,* pp. 14, 15.
9. William James, "The Varieties of Religious Experience," in W. P. Alston, ed., *Religious Belief and Philosophical Thought* (New York: Harcourt, Brace & World, 1963), pp. 130, 136-37.
10. Rudolph Otto, *The Idea of the Holy,* trans. John Harvey (New York: Oxford, Galaxy Books, 1958), pp. 9-11; Martin Buber, *Between I and Thou* (New York: Scribner's, 1970).
11. Donald Walhout, *Interpreting Religion* (Englewood Cliffs, NJ: Prentice-Hall, 1963), pp. 69-71.
12. Bertocci, *Introduction,* p. 66.
13. Ibid., p. 62.
14. Søren Kierkegaard, *Fear and Trembling and The Sickness Unto Death,* trans. Walter Lowrie (New York: Doubleday, Anchor Books, 1958), pp. 31, 44, 49-51, 67.
15. L. Harold DeWolf, *The Religious Revolt Against Reason* (Westport, CT: Greenwood Press, 1968), pp. 203-12.
16. E. S. Brightman, *Philosophy of Religion* (Englewood Cliffs, NJ: Prentice-Hall, 1950), pp. 128-29.
17. Bertocci, *Introduction,* p. 174.

Chapter Three

1. Janheinz Jahn, *Muntu,* trans. Marjorie Grene (New York: Grove Press, 1961). Carlos Castenada, *The Teachings of Don Juan* (Berkeley: University of California Press, 1968).
2. H. N. Wieman, *The Source of Human Good* (Carbondale: Southern Illinois University Press, 1946). C. Lloyd Morgan, *Emergent Evolution* (New York:

Henry Holt and Company, 1923), pp. 292-98. Samuel Alexander, *Space, Time and Deity,* 2 vols. ([1920] New York: Dover, 1966).

3. Heinrich Zimmer, *Philosophies of India,* ed. Joseph Campbell (New York: World Publishing, Meridian Books, 1951), pp. 181 ff.; 217 ff.

4. In keeping with the ecumenical spirit of our study, B.C.E. (before common era) seems more appropriate than B.C. (before Christ); similarly, C.E. (common era) rather than A.D. (year of our Lord).

5. *Ajiva* is composed of five constituent parts: *pudgala* (matter); *akasa* (space); *kala* (time); *dharma* (motion); *adharma* (rest). S. Gopalan, *Outlines of Jainism* (New York: Halsted Press, Division of John Wiley & Sons, 1973), p. 122.

6. I. C. Sharma, *Indian Philosophy: A Critical Survey* (New York: Barnes and Noble, 1962), pp. 157 ff.

7. Ibid., pp. 28 ff.

8. Ibid., ch. 9, pp. 137 ff.

9. Zimmer, *Philosophies of India,* pp. 326-28.

10. S. E. Frost, Jr., *The Sacred Writings of the World's Great Religions* (New York: McGraw Hill, 1972), "The Meng-tze," 2, 1, 6, 1-7 (p. 115); 6, 1.2, 1-3 (pp. 116-17). *See also* Fung Yu-Lan, *A Short History of Chinese Philosophy,* trans. Derk Bodde (New York: Macmillan, 1960), pp. 69 ff.

11. Fung, *Chinese Philosophy,* pp. 65-66. *See also* James Legge, *The Texts of Taoism,* 2 vols., Sacred Books of the East, ed. Max Müller ([1891] New York: Dover, 1962), I:1.

12. Mai-mai Sze, *The Way of Chinese Painting* (New York: Random, Vintage Books, 1959), p. 428. The author has substituted *boat* for *foot* because the battened sail and prominent stern so characteristic of the Chinese junk is clearly apparent to the nautical eye.

13. Legge, *Texts of Taoism,* I:83.

14. Fung, *Chinese Philosophy,* pp. 93, 94.

15. Ibid., ch. 12, pp. 129-42.

16. Carl Jung, *Synchronicity: An Acausal Connecting Principle* (New York: Pantheon, 1955).

17. Fung, *Chinese Philosophy,* pp. 257, 258. *See also* D. T. Suzuki, *Zen Buddhism,* ed. William Barrett (New York: Doubleday, Anchor Books, 1956), pp. 66-68, 157, 158.

18. Suzuki, *Zen Buddhism,* pp. 111 ff.

19. Nancy Ross, *The World of Zen* (New York: Random, 1960), pp. 187-88.

20. Ibid., p. 287.

21. Zimmer, *Philosophies of India,* p. 77, gives a variant account.

22. S. Radhakrishnan, *The Principal Upanishads* ([1953] New York: Humanities Press, 1969), pp. 52-53, 73-74, 77.

23. Zimmer, *Philosophies of India,* pp. 355, 356, 366, 367, 414, 415. *See also The Upanishads,* trans. Swami Prabhavananda and Frederick Manchester (New York: New American Library, Mentor Religious Classic, 1964), esp. the Isha Upanishad (pp. 27 ff.); the Chandogya Upanishad (pp. 64 ff.); the Kaivala Upanishad (pp. 114 ff.).

24. From the Chandogya Upanishad in Prabhavananda, *The Upanishads,* pp. 68-69.

25. Sharma, *Indian Philosophy,* pp. 240 ff.

26. M. Hiriyanna, *Essentials of Indian Philosophy* (London: Allen & Unwin, 1956), pp. 73, 74.

27. Sharma, *Indian Philosophy,* p. 306.

28. Zimmer, *Philosophies of India,* pp. 185, 186 n. 6. *See also* Gopalan, *Outlines of Jainism,* ch. 1, esp. p. 77.

29. E. Conze, ed., *Buddhist Texts through the Ages* (New York: Harper & Row, 1964), p. 10.

30. Zimmer, *Philosophies of India,* p. 527.

31. Sharma, *Indian Philosophy,* pp. 59-60.

32. John M. Koller, *Oriental Philosophies* (New York: Scribner's, 1970), pp. 126 ff. *See also* Conze, *Buddhist Texts,* p. 157 (Mahaprajnaparamita).

33. Conze, *Buddhist Texts,* p. 157.

34. Ibid., pp. 127 ff.

35. S. Radhakrishnan, *History of Philosophy: Eastern and Western,* 2 vols. (London: Allen & Unwin, 1952-53), vol. 1.

36. Kih Pei Yu, or "Knowledge Rambling in the North," in Legge, *Texts of Taoism,* Part 2: "The Writings of Chuang-Tzu," pp. 57-58. "All these names are metaphorical, having more or less to do with the qualities of the Tao" (p. 57 n. 2).

37. Fung, *Chinese Philosophy,* pp. 107-16.

38. Ibid., pp. 109, 110.

39. "How Many Gods?" in Robert O. Ballou, ed., *The Bible of the World* (New York: Viking, 1948), pp. 31, 32.

40. Ibid., p. 54.

41. *The Bhagavad Gita,* trans. Juan Mascaro (New York: Penguin, 1971).

42. J. B. Carman, *The Theology of Ramanuja: An Essay in Interreligious Understanding* (New Haven: Yale University Press, 1974), pp. 158-59.

43. Ibid., p. 192.

44. Radhakrishnan, *The Principal Upanishads,* pp. 130-31.

45. Carman, *Theology of Ramanuja,* p. 124.

46. Sharma, *Indian Philosophy,* pp. 361-63.

47. Koller, *Oriental Philosophies,* pp. 90-91.

48. Grace E. Cairns, *Philosophies of History* (New York: Citadel Press, 1962), pp. 299-306.

49. Sri Aurobindo, *The Life Divine,* 30 vols. (Pondicherry, India: Sri Aurobindo Ashram, 1970), XIX:965 ff., esp. 971, 972, 977, 978.

50. Bernhard Anderson, *Understanding the Old Testament,* 3rd ed. (Englewood Cliffs, NJ: Prentice-Hall, 1975), pp. 35-37.

51. Walter Harrelson, *Interpreting the Old Testament* (New York: Holt, Rinehart and Winston, 1964), pp. 78, 79.

52. Anderson, *Understanding the Old Testament,* pp. 226-29.

53. Robert Pfeiffer, *Introduction to the Old Testament* (New York: Harper Brothers, 1948), pp. 567-60. Pfeiffer argues for Gomer's innocence. *See also* Elmer Leslie, *The Prophets Tell Their Own Story* (Nashville: Abingdon, 1939), pp. 42-45. Leslie offers a counterargument.

54. *See* Isa. 6:3; 7:9*b;* 30:15*a.*

55. Martin Larson, *Religion of the Occident* (Totowa, NJ: Littlefield, Adams & Company, 1961), pp. 95, 102-3, 105.

56. Robert A. Spivey and D. M. Smith, *Anatomy of the New Testament* (London: Macmillan, 1972), pp. 190-94, 201, 211. *See also* James Price, *Interpreting the New Testament,* 2nd ed. (New York: Holt, Rinehart and Winston, 1971), pp. 257-260; and C. Milo Connick, *The New Testament: An Introduction* (Encino, CA: Dickenson Publishing Co., 1972), pp. 118-99; and L. Harold DeWolf, *A Theology of the Living Church,* 2nd rev. ed. (New York: Harper, 1968), pp. 306 ff.

Chapter Four

1. P. A. Bertocci, *Introduction to Philosophy of Religion* (Englewood Cliffs, NJ: Prentice-Hall, 1958), pp. 450-67.
2. Erich Fromm, *Man for Himself* (Greenwich, CT: Fawcett Premier Books, 1965), pp. 102-16.
3. *See* Gen. 18:20-33 where Abram is contesting with Yahweh about the fate of Sodom and Gomorrah.
4. Henri Bergson, "Laughter," in *Comedy* by George Meredith (New York: Doubleday, Anchor Books, 1956), pp. 93, 97, 187-89.
5. *See* Heb. 12.
6. *See* Isa. 52–53 concerning the redemptive power of vicarious suffering and also the Christian doctrine of the Atonement.
7. Willem Zuurdeeg, *An Analytical Philosophy of Religion* (Nashville: Abingdon, 1958), p. 56.
8. Mai-mai Sze, *The Way of Chinese Painting* (New York: Random, Vintage Books, 1959), pp. 431, 432.

Part II

Chapter Five

1. Fung Yu-Lan, *A Short History of Chinese Philosophy,* trans. Derk Bodde (New York: Macmillan, 1960), pp. 138 ff., 169, 269, 270.
2. Ibid., pp. 174, 176 (selection from the *Chung Yung,* ch. 22).
3. John A. Hutchison, *Paths of Faith* (New York: McGraw-Hill, 1969), pp. 170-76.
4. Heinrich Zimmer, *Philosophies of India,* ed. Joseph Campbell (New York: World Publishing, Meridian Books, 1951), p. 527.
5. John B. Noss, *Man's Religions,* 5th ed. (New York: Macmillan, 1974), p. 163.
6. Harold L. DeWolf, *A Theology of the Living Church,* 2nd ed. (New York: Harper, 1968), pp. 276-79.
7. Hutchison, *Paths of Faith,* p. 134; and Noss, *Man's Religions,* p. 163.
8. I. C. Sharma, *Indian Philosophy: A Critical Survey* (New York: Barnes and Noble, 1962), p. 160.
9. *See* Gen. 15:7-21; 17:3-8.
10. *See* Amos 5:24 and Hos. 6:6.
11. Erich Fromm, *Man for Himself* (Greenwich, CT: Fawcett Premier Books, 1965), pp. 104-16.
12. Fung, *Chinese Philosophy,* pp. 16 ff.
13. Robert O. Ballou, ed., *The Bible of the World* (New York: Viking, 1948), pp. 512-23.
14. From "Autumn Floods," ch. 17 of *The Chuang-tzu,* in William DeBarey, ed., *Introduction to Oriental Civilizations: Sources of Chinese Tradition* (New York: Columbia University Press, 1965), pp. 77-78.
15. Fung, *Chinese Philosophy,* p. 114.
16. Nancy Ross, *The World of Zen* (New York: Random, 1960), p. 125.
17. William Dean, *Coming to a Theology of Beauty* (Philadelphia: Westminster, 1972), p. 91.
18. Ibid., pp. 67, 73, 87.

Chapter Six

1. James Legge, *The Texts of Taoism,* 2 vols., Sacred Books of the East, ed. Max Müller ([1891] New York: Dover, 1962), I:47.
2. *See Tao Teh King* 2:3 and 29:1-2 in ibid., I:48 and 71-72.

3. Heinrich Zimmer, *Philosophies of India,* ed. Joseph Campbell (New York: World Publishing, Meridian Books, 1951), p. 281.
4. M. Hiriyanna, *Essentials of Indian Philosophy* (London: Allen & Unwin, 1956), pp. 110-11.
5. Zimmer, *Philosophies of India,* pp. 355, 366, 367.
6. S. Radhakrishnan, *The Principal Upanishads* (Atlantic Highlands, NJ: Humanities Press, 1969), pp. 65 ff.
7. Zimmer, *Philosophies of India,* p. 527.
8. I. C. Sharma, *Indian Philosophy: A Critical Survey* (New York: Barnes and Noble, 1962), pp. 139-40, 171-72.
9. J. B. Carman, *The Theology of Ramanuja: An Essay in Interreligious Understanding* (New Haven: Yale University Press, 1974), pp. 67 ff.
10. Hiriyanna, *Essentials of Indian Philosophy,* pp. 177-78.
11. S. Aurobindo, *The Life Divine* (Pondicherry, India: Sri Aurobindo Ashram, 1970), Book II, Part 2, pp. 964 ff. *See also* Radhakrishnan, *The Principal Upanishads,* pp. 130-31.
12. P. A. Bertocci, *The Person God Is* (Atlantic Highlands, NJ: Humanities Press, 1970), p. 22.
13. Ibid., pp. 25-26.
14. Ibid., p. 27.
15. Ibid., p. 29.
16. Ibid., p. 27.
17. Ramanuja as quoted in P. N. Srinivasachari, *The Philosophy of Visisadvaita,* 2nd ed. (Adyar: Adyar Library, 1946), p. 107, as cited in *ibid.,* p. 233.
18. Ibid., p. 234.
19. Ibid., pp. 234-35.
20. John M. Koller, *Oriental Philosophies* (New York: Scribner's, 1970), p. 92.
21. Bertocci, *The Person God Is,* p. 223.
22. Ibid., p. 236.
23. Ibid., p. 237.

Chapter Seven

1. P. A. Bertocci, *Introduction to Philosophy of Religion* (Englewood Cliffs, NJ: Prentice-Hall, 1958), pp. 59-61.
2. I. C. Sharma, *Indian Philosophy: A Critical Survey* (New York: Barnes and Noble, 1962), p. 271.
3. Ibid., pp. 60-61.
4. Fung Yu-Lan, *A Short History of Chinese Philosophy,* ed. Derk Bodde (New York: Macmillan, 1960), pp. 242-44.
5. S. Radhakrishnan, *The Principal Upanishads* (Atlantic Highlands, NJ: Humanities Press, 1969), pp. 129 ff.
6. S. Aurobindo, *The Life Divine,* 30 vols. (Pondicherry, India: Sri Aurobindo Ashram, 1970), XIX:1019, 1030.
7. *See* Radhakrishnan, *The Principal Upanishads,* p. 131. "In the *brahmaloka* the liberated individuals present to each other as one. . . . Their consciousness of the Supreme which is lodged in the *buddhi* is one and not divided among the bodily forms. This identical consciousness is associated with different bodies. This Manifoldness does not take away from the unity of the divine being." *See also* Aurobindo, *The Life Divine,* p. 1030.

NOTES TO PAGES 167–175

8. M. Hiriyanna, *Essentials of Indian Philosophy* (London: Allen & Unwin, 1956), pp. 189-90.
9. B. P. Bowne, *Principles of Ethics* (New York: Harper & Brothers, 1898), p. 165; and *Personalism* (Boston: Houghton Mifflin, 1908), pp. 200-201, 205-6.
10. D. M. Baillie, *God Was in Christ* (New York: Scribner's, 1948), p. 114.
11. Reinhold Niebuhr, *The Nature and Destiny of Man,* 2 vols. (New York: Scribner's, 1964), I:263.
12. E. S. Brightman, *Person and Reality,* ed. P. A. Bertocci, J. Newhall, and R. S. Brightman (New York: Ronald Press, 1958), pp. 247-48.
13. Ibid., p. 299.
14. E. S. Brightman, *The Moral Laws* (Abingdon, 1933; Kraus Reprint, 1968).
15. E. S. Brightman, *Introduction to the Philosophy of Religion* (Englewood Cliffs, NJ: Prentice-Hall, 1950), pp. 400-401.

Glossary
Some Key Terms from the Religions and Philosophies of the World

Terms from Indian Religious Philosophies

Aham Brahm asmi   "I Am Brahman." Signifying illumination and awareness of mystical unity with Brahman. *See samadhi*

ahimsa   Noninjury: "Thou shalt not kill or harm." *See* Yogic Decalogue

Alaya-vijnana   Buddhist term for ultimate reality—Ground of Being and Consciousness

anatta, or *anatman*   Buddhist doctrine of no permanent self

asatkaryavada   Vaisheshika doctrine of the *not* pre-existent effect—a theory of emergent evolution

Atman   the self or soul of finite persons and also of Brahma

Aurobindo   twentieth-century Indian philosopher

Advaita   nondual, monistic form of Vedanta developed by Shankara

ajiva   matter in Jainism

ananda   bliss

Arhat(or Arahan and Arahanta in the Pali language)   Theravada Buddhist monk

asteya   "Thou shalt not steal." *See* Yogic Decalogue

aparigraha "Thou shalt not covet." *See* Yogic Decalogue

AUM the sacred word expressing mystical experience of Brahman expressed as a dipthong. *See* OM

avidya ignorance, not seeing

Bodhisattva a compassionate Buddha-helper in Mahayana

Brahma the ultimate reality (personal)—first mode of the Trimurti

Brahman the ultimate reality (nonpersonal)

Buddha Gautama's honorific title, "The Enlightened One"

bhakti devotion, faith

bodhi tree the tree under which Buddha was seated when he was enlightened

buddhi intellect, intelligence

brahmacharya "Thou shalt not lust." *See* Yogic Decalogue

Charvaka ancient Dravidian Materialism

chit cosmic consciousness

darshana an intuitive vision of the truth

dharma duty, righteousness

Dharmakaya in Mahayana, Buddha's "Body of Essence," ultimate reality, and the first mode of Trikaya

dhyana meditation—the seventh step in Yoga; epistemic dualism

Dvaita a theistic form of Vedanta developed by Madhva

Gautama Siddhartha Sakyamuni founder of Buddhism

gunas the three qualities of matter; viz., *sattva* (tension or harmony), *rajas* (activity), and *tamas* (inertia)

guru a spiritual teacher

hatha yoga physical discipline for the body

Hinayana the most ancient form of Buddhism of which Theravada is the best known school; literally, the small life raft

Indra a Vedic sky-god

Ishvara   Lord, or God, the personal aspect of Brahman

jiva   spirit, the embodied soul, ego

jivanmukta   one released from *samsara* who experiences *nirvana* while still alive

jnana   consciousness, knowledge; a victor in Jain faith

Jainism   religious philosophy of the Jains

Kali   a consort of Shiva

karma   the effect of action, law of the deed

Krishna   an incarnation of Vishnu; hero of the Gita

karma yoga   Krishna's Yoga of selfless action

lila   eternal delight, divine play of Brahma

Madhva   founder of Dvaita Vedanta

Mahabharata   epic of first-century Hinduism containing the Gita

Mahavira   twenty-fourth and last of Jain Tirthankaras

Mahayana   literally, the big life raft; the idealistic school of later Buddhism

manas   mind, coordinator of sense and motor organs

maya   the illusion of the world

Mimamsa   one of the six systems of Indian philosophy—pluralistic and realistic

moksha   liberation from *samsara*

Narayana   another name for Brahman meaning Supreme Person

Nyaya   one of the six systems of Indian philosophy—a system of logic

nibbana   existence without suffering (the Pali form of *Nirvana*)

Nirmanakaya   "Body of Manifestation" of historical Buddhas; third mode of Trikaya

nirvana   the passionless peace that follows emancipation from *samsara*

neti, neti   "Not that, not that"—denial of any attributes for Brahman

OM   the sacred word expressing mystical experience of Brahman. *See* AUM

Pantanjali   author of the Yoga *sutras*

Prajapati   Lord of Creation in Vedas; the chief god in Hindu henotheism

188

prakrti   primeval matter in Sanhkhya

purusha   primeval spirit in Sankhya; also, soul of a person

pralaya   devolution or collapse of the universe back into matter

pratityasumutpada (or *paticca samuppada* and *satya samutpada* in the Pali language)   Buddhist doctrine of dependent origination; theory of epiphenomalism (everything is dependent on something prior and nothing is permanent)

rajas   one of the three *gunas*: respecting matter, the principle of activity or energy; from the psychological perspective, egoism and selfishness

Rama   an incarnation of Vishnu and hero of the *Ramayana*

Ramanuja   founder of Vishistadvaita

Rig Veda   one of the four ancient Vedas

rasa   the essence, of "flavor," of art and first canon of Indian art

Sama Veda   one of the four Vedas

samsara   eternal cyclic process of the phenomenal universe

satkaryavada   in Sankya, a deterministic theory of evolution that involves reductionism: theory of the pre-existent effect

satya   "Thou shalt not lie." *See* Yogic Decalogue

samadhi   concentration; the eighth and final step in Yoga; epistemic monism

Sambhogakaya   "Body of Bliss," second mode of the Trikaya, Heavenly or Cosmic Buddha

Sankhya   one of the six systems of Indian philosophy—dualistic metaphysics

sat   truth, being

satchitananda (or *saccitananda*)   blissful cosmic consciousness of true being

sattva   one of the three *gunas:* respecting matter, the principle of tension or harmony; from the psychological perspective, purity or fineness

Shankara   founder of Advaita

Sunyata   emptiness, void; a term for the Buddhist Ultimate One

Shiva   Lord of Process: generation and destruction; second mode of the Trimurti

tamas   one of the three *gunas:* respecting matter it is the principle of inertia; from the psychological perspective it is ignorance or passivity

Tat tuam asi   "That thou art"; "You are It," i.e., Brahman

Theravada   early Buddhism. *See* Hinayana

Tirthankara   Jain saint beyond caring

Trikaya   Buddhist Trinity: (1) Darmakaya, (2) Sambhogakaya, (3) Nirmanakaya

Trimurti   Hindu Trinity: (1) Brahma, (2) Vishnu, (3) Shiva

Upanishads   philosophical portion of the Vedas developing monistic metaphysics

Vaisheshika   one of the six systems of Indian philosophy—realistic and pluralistic

Vedanta   one of the six systems of Indian philosophy—monistic and idealistic

Vishistadvaita   a qualified monistic form of Vedanta developed by Ramanuja

Varuna   Vedic ethical sky-god

vidya   to see (vision), to understand

Vishnu   the Lord of Righteousness and Salvation; third mode of the Trimurti

Yoga   one of the six systems of Indian philosophy but also a physical, mental, and moral discipline common to all Eastern religious philosophy: literally, to be "yoked with the truth"

Yogic Decalogue   the *yama:* first stage of Yoga, Thou shalt not—(1) *ahimsa,* harm; (2) *satya,* lie; (3) *asteya,* steal; (4) *brahmacharya,* lust; (5) *aparigraha,* covet

the *niyama:* second stage of Yoga, Thou shalt—(6) *shaucha,* be pure; (7) *santosa,* be content; (8) *tapas,* live simply; (9) *svadhyaya,* study; (10) *ishvarapranidhana,* be devoted to God

Yat sat tat ksanikam   Buddhist doctrine of the flux, process philosophy: "All things are quick as a wink"

Terms from Chinese and Japanese Religious Philosophies

Buddha   the honorific title given to Prince Gautama signifying his enlightenment as founder of Buddhism

Bodhidharma   the legendary missionary who brought Buddhism from India to China

chung-yung   doctrine of the mean, golden rule of *Tao Hsueh:* "Do ordinary things just right"

chung* and *shu   the positive and negative aspects of the golden rule: "Do unto others . . ." and Do *not* do unto others . . ."

Ch'an Buddhism (also Zen)   a school of Buddhism founded by Hui-neng incorporating ideas from Taoism

Ch'ang *the Five Constant Virtues of Neo-Confucianism's personal ethics: (1) jen,* compassion; (2) *yi,* righteousness; (3) *li,* propriety; (4) *chih,* wisdom; (5) *hsin,* good faith

Chuang Tzu; *Chuang-tzu* Taoist mystic philosopher; his book

Ch'i spirit, vital force

Ch'i Yun spirit of the Tao, "rhythmic vitality," first canon of Chinese art

chih wisdom; one of the Four Constant Virtues of Confucianism

chung-yung Doctrine of the Mean

chun-tzu the ideal person, superior man

Fa chia one of the six schools of Chinese philosophy—a system of political philosophy

feng liu Neo-Taoist principle—living according to impulse

feng-shui man must live harmoniously with nature, i.e., "wind and water"

Four Constant Virtues ethics of Confucianism: (1) *jen,* compassion; (2) *yi,* righteousness; (3) *li,* propriety; (4) *chih,* wisdom

ho harmony with the universe, "Supreme Harmony"

Hui-neng founder of Ch'an Buddhism and sixth patriarch of Chinese Buddhism

Hung-jen fifth patriarch of Chinese Buddhism

Hsun Tzu realist philosopher of *Ju chia*

hsiao filial piety

hsin good faith or good will; one of the Five Constant Virtues of Neo-Confucianism

haiku a Japanese poetry style; each poem consists of seventeen syllables

I Ching Book of Changes (one of the five classics). *See Yi Ching*

jen (pronounced *wren*) human-heartedness, compassion, love; one of the Constant Virtues

Ju chia one of the six schools of Chinese philosophy, the one founded by Master Kung; "the scholarly way," Confucianism

kang the five personal relationships of Confucianism's social ethics: (1) sovereign-subject, (2) father-son, (3) husband-wife, (4) elder brother-younger brother, (5) friend-friend

191

K'ung Tzu, or K'ung Fu Tzu   Master K'ung; *Confucius* is Latinized form

koan   problem set for a Zen pupil

Lao Tzu (also Lao Tan, or Li Erh)   philosopher and legendary founder of *Tao-te chia*

Lao-tzu   Lao Tzu's book, later known as *Tao Te Ching* or *Tao Te King*

li   principles, laws, propriety, proper conduct; one of the Constant Virtues

Meng Tzu   greatest disciple of Master K'ung

ming   will of heaven, fate, destiny

Ming chia   one of the six schools of Chinese philosophy—a system of linguistic analysis

Mo chia   one of the six schools of Chinese philosophy—a theistic humanism stressing "all-embracing love" and logic

Pen-lai-wu-i-wu   the first principle of Ch'an Buddhism: "In the beginning there was the void"

p'u   simplicity (of driftwood)

satori   Japanese term for *nirvana* in Zen Buddhism

shu   reciprocity, mutuality

T'ai Chi   the Supreme Ultimate; the trinity of Tao Hsueh: (1) Tao, (2) Yang, (3) Ying

Tao   ultimate reality; the Way of nature and man

Tao Te Ching   text of Taoism, attributed to Lao Tzu

Tao-Te chia   one of the six schools of Chinese philosophy—the philosophy of the Tao

te   the nature of a thing, its power and original virtue

Tao Hsueh   study of philosophy of the Tao; Neo-Confucianism

t'ien   heaven

Trikaya   the Buddhist trinity: (1) Dharmakaya, (2) Sambhogakaya, (3) Nirmana-kaya

tzu jan   natural, naturalness

wu   nonbeing

192

wu hsin   having no mind—the principle of unconsciousness and way of Zen to *satori*

wu hsing   the five powers of *Yin-Yang chia:* (1) water, (2) fire, (3) wood, (4) metal, (5) earth

wu-wei   nonaction, avoidance of artificiality; Taoist golden rule

Yang Chu   earliest Taoist philosopher, who taught a hedonist ethic

yeh   *karma,* deed or action

yi   righteousness; one of the Constant Virtues

Yi Ching   Book of Changes, basic text of *Yin-Yang chia. See I Ching*

yin and yang   female and male principles of the cosmos

Yin-Yang chia   one of the six schools of Chinese philosophy—a dualistic naturalistic philosophy of alternating processes

yu   being

Zen   Japanese Buddhism. *See* Ch'an Buddhism

zazen   discipline of Zen Buddhism

Terms from Western Philosophy

the Absolute   ultimate reality, God

aesthetics   the study of the creation, experience and evaluation of art

agnosticism   a profession of ignorance concerning the existence of God

anthropomorphism   attributing human qualities to the nonhuman real; especially to the nature of God

a posteriori   refers to knowledge gained as a result of having had a particular experience, e.g., fire burns

a priori   refers to knowledge gained by consideration of logical pinciples and independent of any particular experience, e.g., $2 + 2 = 4$

axiology   the study of value, viz., aesthetics, ethics, and philosophy of religion

being   that which exists

cause   that which brings about an effect or a change. Aristotle's four causes: (1) formal, pattern or idea; (2) material, the stuff out of which a thing is made; (3) efficient, the agent or artisan; (4) final, the purpose or goal

coherence   a criterion of truth stressing rational consistency and harmony between ideas and experience

correspondence a criterion of truth stressing identity of idea with objective reality

cosmology the study of the origin, nature, and development of the universe

determinism the theory that nature is a unified system of cause and effect: Humanity, a part of nature, has its actions controlled by previous natural conditions

dialectic theory of reality and/or reasoning that opposites (thesis and antithesis) conflict and are reconciled in a synthesis

dualism the theory that reality consists of two opposing forces (e.g., matter, spirit; good, evil) that cannot be reduced to a common power

emergence, emergent evolution the theory that evolution proceeds in a sequence of new or novel phenomena which cannot be explained or reduced to a lower or previous condition

empiricism all knowledge is *a posteriori* and comes from experience through the five senses

entelechy Aristotle's idea of a nonmaterial force that directs natural processes so that particular forms emerge

epiphenomenalism theory that mind is merely a secondary phenomenon accompanying physical brain activity

epistemic dualism the view that there are two separate entities involved in the knowing process: (1) the subject and his mind and (2) the external object

epistemic monism the view that the knowing subject and object become one in the mystic experience

essence the concept or intrinsic nature of a thing, independent of its existence

ethics the study of the good; systems of moral conduct

evolution the theory that the cosmos with all its orders of existence develops progressively in a rational, orderly manner

existence the state of being in space-time as opposed to mere essence

existentialism an approach to philosophy and theology that stresses human subjectivity, e.g., anxiety about finitude, death, freedom, and creative powers

free will the belief that persons have the power to make at least limited alternative choices: self-determination

humanism an interpretation of the universe and existence based on the worth of humanity and denying the supernatural

194

idealism   an interpretation of existence in terms of ideas in the mind and denying the reality of matter

indeterminism   theory that choices are in some cases free from antecedent causation. *See* free will

instrumental value   anything desired because it can be used to get something else desired

intrinsic value   anything having worth in itself and desired for its own sake

intuitionism   the view that knowledge can be gained by direct apprehension and is not the result of conscious reasoning but may be related to sense perception

logical positivism   a philosophy asserting that knowledge is limited to scientifically verifiable matters and propositions verifiable by analysis of the definitions of the terms

logical laws   the basic laws of thought which structure all discursive thinking: (1) principle of identity, (2) principle of noncontradiction, (3) principle of excluded middle

materialism   a system of philosophy asserting that matter alone is real and life and mind are only manifestations of it

mechanism   the theory that nature is to be understood in terms of determinate principles

meliorism   the view that the world is neither entirely good or evil but can be improved by human effort

metaphysics   the study of the nature of ultimate reality

monism   the belief that there is only one fundamental reality, e.g., mind, nature, energy, pure potentiality

naturalism   the view that nature is the whole of reality and should be studied empirically; supernaturalism is rejected

nature   the system of all phenomena in space-time

ontology   the study of the nature of being and a branch of metaphysics

person   a being that is self-conscious, capable of thinking and making ethical choices and capable of enjoying and creating other values

personalism   a philosophy asserting that reality is to be understood as a community of persons, finite and divine, possessing intrinsic worth and that the environing nature exists as instrumental value for them

pluralism   the view that reality is manifold, in contrast with monism and dualism

pragmatism   the philosophy that understands reality in terms of experience: truth is discovered by experimental inquiry and verified if it works

rationalism   the view that the mind can gain knowledge independent of sense experiences, i.e., *a priori* knowledge

reason   the capacity to think reflectively and draw conclusions

self   the person or principle of unity that persists through change, the subject "I" and "me"

validity   formal correctness of an argument independent of the truth or falseness of the premises

value   anything desired, prized, or regarded as having worth

verification   truth testing an assertion by means of some procedure, e.g., coherence, practical results, correspondence

Terms Used in Biblical Religion and Theology

agape   the unmerited, unselfish, spontaneous, and creative love of God

apocalypticism   a supernatural view of the end of the world stressing God's intervention and dramatic events

agnosticism   the position that we can never know whether or not God exists

atheism   the denial that God exists

Baal   the male Canaanite fertility god whose consort is Ashtart

being-itself   Tillich's term for ultimate reality, or God

biblical criticism   the scholarly study of biblical literature, including textual, literary, source, form, and redaction criticism

biblical theology   theology based on ideas found in and doctrines drawn from biblical literature

Christ, or *Christos*   the Greek honorific title for Jesus meaning messiah, or "annointed one"

Christology   theories about the person and works of Jesus Christ, e.g., incarnation and atonement

cosmological argument   an argument for the existence of God based on the recognition of the cosmos and the need for a first cause to explain its existence

deity   a word meaning God or identity with God, e.g., the deity of Jesus Christ, i.e., his nature is *homoousios* (identical), to the nature of God

divine   a word meaning God-like, e.g., the divinity of Jesus Christ, i.e., his nature is *homoiousios* (similar) to the nature of God

Deuteronomic philosophy of history   the view attributed to the Deuteronomic

196

("D") redactor that piety and impiety are respectively rewarded by good and bad fortune

demonic   wicked, evil behavior attributed to the Devil or the base urges in humans

Devil, or Satan   the principle of evil, either a literal supernatural person or a symbol to be metaphorically understood

demythologize   Bultmann's term for discovering the existential meaning of religious language apart from its mythological setting

evil and the problem of evil   evil is that which frustrates the realization of the good. The problem of evil is concerned with explaining the presence of moral and natural evil and the suffering entailed in a universe created by and presided over by a good, all-powerful God

El   the supreme father-god of the Canaanite pantheon. The term became linked with patriarchal religion, e.g., El Roi

eschaton   the Greek work for "end," as in "end of the world"

eschatology   theory about the end of the world; there are three main theories: (1) futuristic eschatology, the end is yet to come and will be an outward supernatural event; (2) realized eschatology, the theory propounded by C. H. Dodd that the "end time" began coming with Jesus' ministry and continues to come as we do God's will, an immanentalist view; (3) an attempt to combine the above views: the kingdom is coming immanently but the conclusion will be apocalyptic

Elohim   the plural form of El and the name for God in The "E" document

El Berith   God of the Covenant

El Olam   Everlasting God

El Roi   God who sees

El Shaddai   God of the mountains, or God Almighty

exegesis   the critical interpretation of a text to try to find its meaning

eternity   endless time, cosmic and also at the level of human experience

finite-infinite God   a term suggested by E. S. Brightman to explain natural evil, which means that God is perfect in goodness but limited in power

foreknowledge   the doctrine that because God is omniscient, he knows all future events

foreordination   the doctrine that the omnipotent God has already willed all future events

form criticism (from German *formgeschichte*)   an attempt to identify the history of the evolving forms of oral tradition to better understand the written text

formal sin   an act contrary to God's will and known to be such

Fourth Gospel   Gospel of John

fundamentalism   a theological orientation characterized by biblical literalism and a general antipathy toward the modern scientific method and world view

God   the ultimate being and creator of the universe interpreted in some way as being a Person, personal, or the ground of personality

Heilsgeschichte   literally, holy or salvation history; the idea that divine providence guides the course of history to the end of revealing and achieving God's plan of salvation

holy   pertaining to the nature of God; above and beyond human understanding and eliciting awe and worship

hell   the place or condition of punishment and torment for evil doers; alienation from God

immanent   the idea that God dwells and works within the world of nature and persons

imminent   about to occur; as concerning the imminent end of the world

Incarnation   the doctrine that Jesus Christ was the human embodiment of the Spirit of God

infinite   unlimited in all respects, e.g., the infinite power of God

Jesus Christ   the first-century Jewish rabbi from Nazareth and founder of Christianity whose followers believe him to be the promised messiah, or Christ

habiru, **or** *'apiru*   the Semitic word meaning desert wanderer or outcast and perhaps "Hebrew"

Hasidim   the pious folk of ancient Israel

hubris (from Greek *hybris*)   overbearing pride

kenosis **theory**   Paul's doctrine of the Incarnation explaining that God "emptied" *(kenosis)* himself of his omnipowers and took on finite human form

kerygma   the Greek word meaning the central theme of the gospels, i.e., Jesus is the Christ

kingdom of God   the ideal community of ethical love, presided over by God and founded on his power and righteousness

liberalism   a theological orientation in which biblical interpretation is guided by reason and experience and is generally in harmony with the scientific world view

love   the key word for understanding the Christian message about God acting on humanity's behalf. In I John, God is defined as love. There are three main categories of love in Greek thought: (1) *agape* ($\alpha\gamma\alpha\pi\eta$), unselfish giving love of God; (2) *philia* ($\phi\iota\lambda\iota\alpha$), a reciprocal, brotherly love, or friendship; (3) *eros* ($\epsilon\rho o s$), desiring, craving love, or passion

life after death, or immortality   the doctrine that the soul continues to live after the death of the body

logos   Greek for "word"; in Christian texts, $\lambda o \gamma o s$, Word, or the "creative wisdom and power of God," e.g., "In the beginning was the Word" (John 1:1)

material sin   an act contrary to God's will but committed in ignorance

messiah   a person chosen and annointed by God to perform a special task, e.g., restore Israel, redeem mankind, bring in the kingdom of God. *See* Christ

monotheism   the belief that there is only one God

mysticism   unity with nature, God, or reality is possible and the only path to true knowledge

myth   a nonliteral story that symbolically represents deepest human intuitions concerning destiny and the meaning of life

neo-orthodoxy   a theological interpretation that attempts to recover the significant ideas of Christian theology allegedly discarded by liberalism through the application of psychological insights, existential philosophy, linguistic analysis, and a new supernatural world view

numen   a Latin term signifying God, approximating the Greek term $\delta\epsilon\iota\nu o s$, or terrible, wierd, and beyond all rational categories of thought

numinous   the adjectival form of *numen,* i.e., the holy power of God that causes us to feel "creaturely"

Original Sin   the doctrine that when Adam disobeyed God's command all humankind fell from grace, or in the tradition of Augustine, the interpretation of sin as hubris, or overweening pride in every person

ontological argument   the argument for the existence of God based on the unique meaning and linguistic function of the word *God*

paraclete   the "Comforter," or Holy Spirit of God, which comes to Christians and takes the place of a literal, physical second coming of Christ at the end of this age; an idea found in the Fourth Gospel

parousia   the literal, physical second coming of Christ at the end of this age; an idea found in the synoptic gospels. *See* eschatology and apocalypticism

polytheism   the belief that there are many gods

predestination   *see* foreordination

prophet   one who speaks for God; the emphasis should be on *forth*telling rather than *fore*telling (Hebrew, *nabi*)

Resurrection   the doctrine that Jesus Christ rose from the dead either physically or in spirit according to two different traditions in the synoptic gospels

sin   any act or thought contrary to the will of God. *See* formal sin and material sin

soul   the source of the spiritual life sometimes conceived as mind, personal consciousness, or personality

synoptic gospels   the first three gospels, Matthew, Mark, and Luke; so called because of their relatively similar view of the life and teachings of Jesus

telos   the Greek word for "end"

teleology   theory, or explanation, of history or creation based on the premise that God has a purpose or end in view

teleological argument   the argument for God based on evidence that nature seems to have been designed to achieve a goal or purpose

theology   the study of God, his relation to the world and persons, and the system of beliefs or doctrines relevant

Torah   the Pentateuch, first five books of the Bible, "The Law"

Trinity   an interpretation of ultimate reality that identifies the divine power in three dimensions of activity and human experience. The Christian Trinity: God is (1) Father, (2) Son, and (3) Holy Spirit. *See* Trikaya, Trimurti, and T'ai Chi

universe   the totality of all being in space-time

Ungrund   a German term for metaphysical ground of all being, i.e., God

Weltanschauung   a German term meaning world view: belief about the universe, its meaning and humanity's place in it.

Bibliography

Scriptures of the Religions of the World

Ballou, Robert O. *et al.,* eds. *The Bible of the World.* Viking Press, N.Y., 1948.

Buttrick, George, and Harmon, Nolan B., eds. *The Interpreter's Bible.* 12 vols. Abingdon Cokesbury Press, New York, 1952.

Conze, Edward *et al.,* eds. *Buddhist Texts Through the Ages.* New York: Harper and Row, Torchbooks, 1964.

Frost, S. E., Jr., ed. *The Sacred Writings of the World's Great Religions.* New York: McGraw-Hill, 1972.

Lao-Tze. *Canon of Reason and Virtue.* Translated by Paul Carus. Rev. ed. (original title: *Tao Teh King*). La Salle, IL: Open Court, 1964

Legge, James, trans. *The Texts of Taoism: The Sacred Books of China.* 2 vols. New York: Dover Publications, 1962.

Lin Yutang. *The Wisdom of Confucius.* New York: Random House, Modern Library, 1938.

Mascaro, Juan, trans. *The Bhagavad Gita.* New York: Penguin, 1971.

Müller, F. Max, ed. *The Sacred Books of the East.* 50 vols. trans. by various Oriental scholars. Delhi, Montilal, Banarsidass, 1962-69.

Prabhavananda, Swami, and Manchester, Frederick, trans. *The Upanishads: Breath of the Eternal.* New York: New American Library, Mentor Religious Classic, 1964.

Radhakrishnan, S. *The Principal Upanishads.* New York: Humanities Press, 1969.

The Common Bible (Revised Standard Version). New York: Thomas Nelson & Sons, 1973.

Waley, Arthur, trans. *The Analects of Confucius.* [1938] New York: Humanities, 1964.

Studies of Individual Traditions

Anderson, Bernhard. *Understanding the Old Testament.* 3rd ed. Englewood Cliffs, NJ: Prentice-Hall, 1975.

Aurobindo, Sri. *The Life Divine,* Book Two, Part Two, vol. 19, Birth Centenary Library. Pondicherry, India: Sri Aurobindo Ashram, 1970.

Bernard, Theos. *Indian Philosophy.* New York: Philosophical Library, 1947.

Carman, J. B. *The Theology of Ramanuja: An Essay in Interreligious Understanding.* New Haven: Yale University Press, 1974.

Connick, C. Milo. *The New Testament: An Introduction to its History, Literature, and Thought.* Encino, CA: Dickerson Publishing, 1972.

Dasgupta, Surendranath. *A History of Indian Philosophy.* 5 vols. New York: Cambridge University Press, 1955.

DeBary, William T. *Introduction to Oriental Civilization.* 3 vols. Sources of Indian, Chinese, and Japanese Tradition. New York: Columbia University Press, 1965.

Doty, William. *Contemporary New Testament Interpretation.* Englewood Cliffs, NJ: Prentice-Hall, 1972.

Fung Yu-Lan. *A History of Chinese Philosophy.* 2 vols. Translated by Derk Bodde. New York: Macmillan, 1960.

———. *A Short History of Chinese Philosophy.* Translated by Derk Bodde. New York: Macmillan, 1960.

Gopalan, S. *Outlines of Jainism.* New York: Halsted Press, a division of John Wiley & Sons, 1973.

Harrelson, Walter. *Interpreting the Old Testament.* New York: Holt, Rinehart & Winston, 1964.

Hiriyanna, M. *Essentials of Indian Philosophy.* London: Allen & Unwin, 1956.

Jahn, Janheinz. *Muntu.* Translated by Marjorie Grene. New York: Grove Press, 1961.

Koller, John M. *Oriental Philosophies.* New York: Scribner's, 1970.

Larson, Martin. *Religion of the Occident.* New York: Littlefield Adams, 1961.

Leslie, Elmer K. *The Prophets Tell Their Own Story.* Nashville: Abingdon Cokesbury, 1939.

Mai-mai Sze. *The Way of Chinese Painting: Its Ideas and Technique.* New York: Vintage Books, 1959.

Mould, Elmer. *Essentials of Bible History.* New York: Ronald Press, 1951.

Pfeiffer, Robert. *Introduction to the Old Testament.* New York: Harper and Brothers, 1948.

Price, James. *Interpreting the New Testament.* 2nd. ed. New York: Holt, Rinehart and Winston, 1971.

Radhakrishnan, S. *Indian Philosophy.* 2nd ed. 2 vols. Atlantic Highlands, NJ: Humanities Press, 1962.

Ross, Nancy. *The World of Zen.* New York: Random House, 1960.

Schweitzer, Albert. *Indian Thought and Its Development.* Translated by Mrs. Charles Russell. Boston: Beacon Press, 1960.

Sharma, I. C., and Daugert, Stanley M. *Ethical Philosophies of India.* Lincoln, NB: Johnsen Publishing, 1965.

Spirey, Robert, and Smith, D. M., Jr. *Anatomy of the New Testament.* New York: 1972.

Suzuki, D. T. *Zen Buddhism.* Edited by William Barrett. New York: Doubleday Anchor Books, 1956.

Tomlin, E. W. F. *The Oriental Philosophers.* New York: Harper Colophon Books, 1967.

Watts, Alan W. *The Way of Zen.* New York: Random, Vintage Books, 1965.

Zimmer, Heinrich. *Philosophies of India.* Edited by Joseph Campbell. New York: World Publishing, Meridian Books, 1951.

Theology and Philosophy of Religion

Abernethy, George L., and Langford, Thomas A., eds. *Philosophy of Religion: A Book of Readings.* 2nd ed. New York: Macmillan, 1971.

Alston, William P. *Religious Belief and Philosophical Thoughts.* New York: Harcourt, Brace, Jovanovich, 1963.

Baillie, Donald. *God Was in Christ.* New York: Scribner's, 1948.

Bertocci, Peter. *Introduction to the Philosophy of Religion.* Englewood Cliffs, NJ: Prentice-Hall, 1958.

———. *The Person God Is.* Atlantic Highlands, NJ: Humanities Press, 1970.

Brightman, E. S. *The Moral Laws.* Nashville: Abingdon-Cokesbury, 1933; Kraus Reprint, 1968.

———. *Philosophy of Religion,* Prentice-Hall, New York, 1950.

———. *Person and Reality.* Edited by P. A. Bertocci, J. Newhall, and R. S. Brightman. New York: Ronald Press, 1958.

Brown, Delwin; James, Ralph; and Reeves, Gene. *Process Philosophy and Christian Thought.* New York: Bobbs-Merrill, 1971.

Buber, Martin. *I and Thou.* New York: Scribner's, 1970.

Bultmann, Rudolph. *Kerygma and Myth.* Edited by Hans W. Bartsch and translated by Reginald H. Fuller. New York: Harper, 1966.

Cobb, John B. *Living Options in Protestant Theology.* Philadelphia: Westminster, 1962.

DeWolf, L. Harold. *Responsible Freedom.* New York: Harper, 1971.

———. *The Religious Revolt Against Reason.* Westport, CT: Greenwood Press, 1968.

———. *A Theology of the Living Church.* 2nd ed. New York: Harper, 1968.

Diamond, Malcolm. *Contemporary Philosophy and Religious Thought.* New York: McGraw-Hill, 1974.

Ferré, Frederick. *Basic Modern Philosophy of Religion.* New York: Scribner's, 1967.

———. *Language, Logic and God.* New York: Harper, 1961.

Hick, John. *Classical and Contemporary Readings in Philosophy of Religion.* 2nd ed. Englewood Cliffs, NJ: Prentice-Hall, 1970.

Horden, William. *A Layman's Guide to Protestant Theology.* Rev. ed. New York: Macmillan, 1968.

Hughes, Philip. *Creative Minds in Contemporary Theology.* 2nd rev. ed. Grand Rapids, Michigan: Eerdman's, 1969.

Kierkegaard, Søren. *Fear and Trembling and The Sickness Unto Death.* Translated by Walter Lowrie. New York: Doubleday Anchor Books, 1955.

Miller, L., ed. *Philosophical and Religious Issues.* Encino, CA: Dickenson Publishing Company, 1971.

Morgan, Lloyd. *Emergent Evolution.* New York: Henry Holt, 1923.

Nicholls, William. *Systematic and Philosophical Theology.* Vol. 1 of Pelican Guide to Modern Theology. New York: Penguin Books, 1969.

Niebuhr, Reinhold. *The Nature and Destiny of Man.* 2 vols. New York: Scribner's, 1964.

Otto, Rudolph. *The Idea of the Holy.* Translated by John Harvey. New York: Oxford University Press, Galaxy Books, 1958.

Tillich, Paul. *Systematic Theology.* 3 vols. Chicago: University of Chicago Press, 1951-63.

Trueblood, Elton. *Philosophy of Religion.* New York: Harper, 1957.

Walhout, Donald. *Interpreting Religion.* Englewood Cliffs, NJ: Prentice-Hall, 1963.

Zuurdeeg, Willem. *An Analytical Philosophy of Religion.* Nashville: Abingdon, 1958.

Comparative Religion

Bowker, John. *Problems of Suffering in the Religions of the World.* London: Cambridge University Press, 1970.

Campbell, Joseph. *The Masks of God: Oriental Mythology.* New York: Viking, 1962.

Chan, W., and Alfaguri, I. R. *The Great Asian Religions.* New York: Macmillan, 1969.

Dye, James W., and Forthman, William H. *Religions of the World.* New York: Irvington, 1967.

Eliade, Mircea. *Patterns in Comparative Religion.* Translated by Rosemary Sheed. New York: World Publishing, Meridian Books, 1966.

Hick, John, ed. *Truth and Dialogue in World Religions.* Philadelphia: Westminster Press, 1974.

Hocking, W. E. *The Coming World Civilization.* New York: Harper, 1956.

Moore, Charles, ed. *Philosophy East and West.* Freeport, N.Y.: Princeton University Press, Books for Libraries Press, Early Index Reprint Series, 1970.

Northrop, F. S. C. *The Meeting of East and West.* New York: Macmillan, 1958.

Noss, John. *Man's Religions.* 5th ed. New York: Macmillan, 1974.

Otto, Rudolph. *Mysticism East and West.* Translated by Bertha Bracey and Richenda Payne. New York: Macmillan, Collier Books, 1962.

Radhakrishnan, S. *East and West in Religion.* London: Allen & Unwin, 1958.
———. *Eastern Religions and Western Thought.* New York: Macmillan, 1958.

Raju, P. T. *Introduction to Comparative Philosophy.* Lincoln, NB: University of Nebraska Press, Aretures Books, 1970.

Schweitzer, Albert. *The Philosophy of Civilization.* New York: Macmillan, 1960.

Slater, R. L. *World Religions and World Community.* New York: Columbia University Press, 1963.

Smart, Ninian. *The Religious Experience of Mankind.* New York: Scribner's, 1969.

Dictionaries and Grammars

Chinese
Chiang Yee. *Chinese Calligraphy.* New York: Methuen & Co., 1938.

Dawson, Raymond. *An Introduction to Classical Chinese.* Oxford: Clarendon Press, 1968.

Forrest, R. A. D. *The Chinese Language.* 2nd ed. Farber & Farber, 1965.

German
Bruel, Karl. *Cassell's New German and English Dictionary.* Edited by Harold T. Betteridge. New York: Funk and Wagnalls, 1965.

Greek
Fobes, Francis. *Philosophical Greek.* Chicago: University of Chicago Press, 1966.

Jones, Henry, ed. *Greek English Lexicon.* Oxford: Clarendon Press, 1966.

Machen, J. Gresham. *New Testament Greek for Beginners.* New York: Macmillan, 1950.

Hebrew
Greenberd, Moshy. *Introduction to Hebrew.* Englewood Cliffs, NJ: Prentice-Hall, 1965.

Lambdin, Thomas. *Introduction to Biblical Hebrew.* New York: Scribner's, 1971.

Yates, Kyle. *The Essentials of Biblical Hebrew.* Revised by John Owens. New York: Harper, 1954.

Latin

Latham, R. E., ed. *Revised Latin Word List*. London: Oxford University Press, 1973.

Sanskrit

Gonda, Jan. *A Concise Elementary Grammar of the Sanskrit Language*. Translated by Gordon Ford. London: E. J. Brill, 1966.

Perry, Edward. *A Sanskrit Primer*. New York: Columbia University Press, 1965.

Index

DATE